AFRICAN-AMERICAN
VOICES

AFRICAN-
AMERICAN
VOICES

/\.\./\

EDITED AND WITH
INTRODUCTIONS AND NOTES BY
MICHELE STEPTO

/\.\./\

Writers of America
THE MILLBROOK PRESS
BROOKFIELD, CONNECTICUT

Photographs courtesy of The Schomburg Center: pp. 15, 52–53;
Collection of Roger R. Ricco, photo courtesy of the Maresca
Gallery, N.Y.: p. 33; Collection of Reba and Dave Williams: pp. 69,
85, 124, 144–145; Museum of Fine Arts, Boston: p. 76; Estate
of Romare Bearden: pp. 109, 137; Houston Museum of Fine Arts:
p. 112; Hampton University Museum, Hampton, Va.: p. 130.

Library of Congress Cataloging-in-Publication Data
African-American voices / edited by Michele Stepto.
p. cm.—(Writers of America)
Summary: A collection of writings by such authors as W.E.B.
Du Bois, Toni Morrison, Rita Dove, Richard Wright, and Ralph Ellison,
exploring the connections of circle, veil, water, and song that link
past and present African American cultures.
ISBN 1-56294-474-6
1. Children's literature, American—Afro-American authors.
2. Afro-Americans—Literary collections. [1. Afro-Americans—
Literary collections. 2. American literature—Afro-American
authors—Collections.] I. Stepto, Michele. II. Series.
PZ5.A249 1995
810.8'09281'08996073—dc20 94-16081 CIP AC

Published by The Millbrook Press, Inc.
2 Old New Milford Road
Brookfield, Connecticut 06804

For Robert

Contents

Preface

This is a book about the African-American literary tradition and some of the voices that have been raised within it. What is a literary tradition? It is a way of *saying* as well as *seeing*. It is a habit of caring about certain moments in history and in life.

Like other traditions, a literary tradition is made up of certain practices that give meaning and purpose to those who work within it. Like other traditions, a literary tradition both confines and liberates its members. It keeps their work within certain boundaries, as a riverbank confines the water to its course, but it also makes their words run deep with other words and other meanings that writers before them have used.

Not all African-American writers belong to the African-American literary tradition, but a surprising number of them have written within it, producing a literature of astonishing power and beauty.

Michele Stepto
New Haven, 1994

AFRICAN-AMERICAN VOICES

Introduction

SLAVERY, CULTURE, AND THE BEGINNINGS OF A LITERATURE

The history of African Americans in the United States begins in 1619. In that year, twenty Africans were brought in a Dutch warship into the harbor of Jamestown, Virginia, and sold from there into servitude. They had been captured on the high seas when Dutch sailors overtook and boarded a Spanish slaver bound for the West Indies.

In one respect, these twenty people were lucky. Slavery was already well established in the West Indies, whereas the new Virginia colony relied on "indentures," or contract servitude, for its labor force. This meant that some or all of those twenty people served out their labor contracts and were made freemen. Once free, they may have settled down in the new colony, acquiring land and servants of their own, or they may have gone elsewhere, perhaps even back to West Africa.

Africans who came after them were not so lucky. In 1641, twenty-two years after the Dutch slaver entered the Jamestown harbor, racial slavery was legalized in the Massachusetts Colony. By 1700, virtually all Africans in every one of the American colonies were held in bondage. And as the colonies expanded and the need for labor grew, more and more Africans turned up for sale in slave markets from Boston to Charleston.

Half of all the African people brought forcibly to North America arrived during the forty years just prior to the American Revolution. Few ever saw their homeland again. Slavery as practiced in the American colonies held them for life. And because laws everywhere defined slavery as a hereditary condition passed down from enslaved mother to child, slavery also held their children. For this reason, as the years went by, newly arriving Africans joined a growing community of African Americans who had been born into slavery on American shores.

Enslaved together in towns and cities and farms, large and small, up and down colonial North America, Africans and African Americans engaged in an extraordinary exchange of cultural information. African Americans assisted recently arrived Africans in countless ways, helping them to adjust to a new land and language and to their new condition as enslaved laborers.

Africans in turn brought with them the stories and poems, the music and dance and song, the symbols, the values, the spiritual vision of their distant communities, in this way continually freshening the African roots of African-American culture. When Congress outlawed the Atlantic slave trade in 1808, the importation of African labor ceased, and this long exchange came to an end, but not before it had created a vibrant culture that wedded the African past to the American present.

Kneeling Slave, by nineteenth-century printmaker and draftsman Patrick Reason.

Slavery was legal for more than two hundred years, from 1641 until the passage of the 13th Amendment to the Constitution in 1865. During that time, it exercised almost complete control over the labor, mobility, and progeny of most African Americans. Enslaved men and women still shaped the world around them, however. In art and song, in religious practice and domestic craft, they infused their lives with hope and meaning, at the same time generously enriching the cultural life of other Americans.

While African Americans did not begin to publish their own writings until the mid-1700s, the African-American literary tradition began in 1619 with the arrival in Jamestown of the Dutch ship and its twenty Africans. In the stories and songs that they and succeeding generations first carried to America, enslaved people told the truth of their condition, often in a way only they understood. Passed down through family and community, such stories and songs have provided a valuable legacy for later African-American writers. Along with that legacy has come the theme of exile, of permanent separation from a better place and time, of intense yearning for home and kin.

The long campaign to abolish slavery also left its mark on African-American writing. Following the Revolutionary War, the northern states gradually abolished slavery, but it took even firmer root in the South. Slaveholders defended their interests on the grounds that slaves were "contented" and that slavery itself was "civilizing." Such arguments were especially self-serving given antiliteracy laws, intended to prevent enslaved people from learning to read and write. They learned anyway, often in secret, and used their hard-won literacy to expose the truth about slavery. Like the enslaved singer and storyteller, who spoke in coded language of the brutalities of slavery and the hope of freedom, early African-American writers, many of them fugitive slaves, countered the slaveholders' lies. In narrative, commentary, and public address, they helped to bring about the end of slavery.

The urgent need to record events truthfully animates all African-American writing, the powerful lesson of an enslaved past. Whenever other Americans have tried to deny certain ugly truths—the injustice of slavery, the horror of racial violence, the existence of discrimination—African-American voices have been raised to set the record straight.

Today, African-American writers continue to record the truth as they see it, knowing that if they do not, no one else will. They continue to find inspiration in a culture of song and storytelling as well as in a tradition of African-American writing now more than 250 years old. As modern scholarship unearths more and more information about the past, the connections between early and present African-American culture become ever clearer, and writers discover new inspiration in materials previously lost to memory.

The passages in this book have been selected to illustrate four such connections, those having to do with the circle and the veil, with water and with song. Their meaning and importance will become clearer to you as you read on. They may appear as metaphors, as ideas, or as symbols, but think of them first as connections that unite African-American writers of different times and regions within a single tradition of thought and expression.

PART ONE

CIRCLE
AND VEIL

/\/\/\

THE SACRED CIRCLE: GEOMETRY OF CONNECTIONS

Walk together, children . . .
Sing together, children . . .
Shout together, children . . .
Don't you get weary.

—Spiritual

I was standing by my window
On one cold and cloudy day
When I saw the hearse come rolling
To take my baby away.

Will the circle be unbroken?
By and by, by and by.
There's a greater love awaiting
In the sky, Lord, in the sky.

—Blues

Of all the connections uniting African-American writers, the circle reaches farthest back into the African past. More than a simple connection, it is itself a symbol of connection.

West Africans brought with them from their distant communities a complex worldview in which they the living were united with gods, ancestors, and those still unborn in a vast circle of human meaning and obligation. As the sun moved in a circle, each night entering the unseen world, so people entered an unseen world at death. The first to enter that world were the gods, who taught succeeding generations how to honor their ancestors with offerings and in dance and other forms of worship. Thus honored, the ancestors in turn brought about the birth of new children and endowed the community with spiritual and material gifts.

Without the ancestors' protection, the community would perish. Even so, without the community, the individual must die. Thus, the struggle of West Africans in the American colonies to form new communities was for them a matter of life and death. The slave trade had torn them from towns and villages up and down West Africa and jumbled them together in slave forts and slave ships. They spoke different languages and had different customs, yet a spiritual outlook united them. They shared a reverence for the ancestors, and shared as well certain ways of honoring them, including the circle dance, or ring shout, as it came to be called.

The ring shout was widely practiced in early African-American funeral ceremonies. Moving together in a circle, slowly at first and then faster and faster, singing and shouting and clapping hands, African men and women helped the dead enter the world of the ancestors, in this way redrawing the sacred circle of humanity in the soil of the New World.

When they converted to Christianity, Africans brought the ring shout into their Christian worship. Over the years, however, as African culture became African-American culture, the sacred meanings of the circle dance became lost or obscured. More and more, it began to strike many African Americans as primitive. Fewer and fewer people engaged in it, and then only in secret. Writing in 1925, James Weldon Johnson remembered the secret dances in the church of his boyhood:

> . . . the "ring shout" was looked upon as a very questionable form of worship. It was distinctly frowned upon by a great many colored people. Indeed, I do not recall ever seeing a "ring shout" except *after* the regular services. Almost whispered invitations would go around, "Stay after church; there's going to be a 'ring shout.' " The more educated ministers and members, as fast as they were able to brave the primitive element in the churches, placed a ban on the "ring shout."

Although the circle dance, or ring shout, is rare now, the African circle survives. We recognize it in the blues lyrics at the head of this chapter, and we encounter it again and again in the writing of African Americans, where it remains a sacred symbol of community,

The meaning of this circle has been complicated in the American world, where African culture has been held in contempt, and where membership in the African-American community has too often meant misery and shame. In writers as far apart as Frederick Douglass and Andrea Lee, the circle has gathered to itself all of the discomfort and unease people have felt in a world hostile to their African heritage.

This brief tale, first published in a 1928 collection of African-American stories, has roots deep in slavery and the African past. It concerns Bur Rabbit, or Brer Rabbit, as he is sometimes called, a trickster figure whose stories and legends traveled with West Africans to the Americas. In many of these stories, Bur Rabbit cleverly triumphs over stronger, bigger animals. Here, Bur Rabbit leads a ring shout of the "little birds an' beasts" in a deserted churchyard. The writing here reproduces the original storyteller's South Carolinian speech.

BUR RABBIT IN RED HILL CHURCHYARD

I pass 'long one night by Red Hill churchyard an' I hear all kind er chune. I stop an' look an' my eye like to jump out er my head at wha' I see. De ground was kiver all over wid snow, an' de palin's on de graveyard fence was cracklin', it been so cold. De moon was shinin' bright—mighty nigh like day. De only diff'ence been it ain' look as natu'al. An' I look an' listen—an' ain' nothin' been de matter wid my eye an' ain' nothin' been wrong wid my hearin'—an' I seen a rabbit settin' on top of a grave playin' a fiddle, for God's sake. All kind er little beasts been runnin' 'round, dancin' an' callin' numbers. An' dere was wood rats an' squirrels cuttin' capers wid dey fancy self, an' diff'ent kind er birds an' owl. Even dem ole owl was sachayin' 'round—look like dey was enjoyin' dey self. An' dat ole rabbit was puttin' on more airs dan a poor buckra [white] wid a jug er liquor an' a new suit er clothes on.

Well, sir, I jes stood der wid my heart in my mout' an' my

eyes bu'stin' out my head. I been natu'ally paralyze, I been so scared. An' while I were lookin', Bur Rabbit stop playin', put he fiddle under he arm an' step off de grave. He walk off a little piece an' guin some sort er sign to de little birds an' beasts, an' dey form dey self into a circle 'round de grave. An' dat was when I knowed sump'n strange was guh happen.

You know a rabbit is cunnin'. He got more sense dan people. He sharp. My brother, he ain' trust no mistake.

Well, I watch an' I see Bur Rabbit take he fiddle from under he arm an' start to fiddlin' some more, an' he were doin' some fiddlin' out dere in dat snow. An' Bur Mockin' Bird jine him an' whistle a chune dat would er made de angels weep. Even dem ole owl had tear drappin' from dey eye. Dat mockin' bird an' dat rabbit—Lord, dey had chunes floatin' all 'round on de night air. Dey could stand a chune on end, grab it up an' throw it away an' ketch it an' bring it back an' hold it; an' make dem chunes sound like dey was strugglin' to git away one minute, an' de next dey sound like sump'n gittin' up close an' whisperin'.

An' as I watch, I see Bur Rabbit lower he fiddle, wipe he face an' stick he han'k'ch'ef in he pocket, an' take off he hat an' bow mighty nigh to de ground. Bur Mockin' Bird stop he chune an' all de little beasts an' birds an' dem ole owl bow down.

An' wuh you reckon? While I been watch all dese strange guines on, I see de snow on de grave crack an' rise up, an' de grave open an' I see Simon rise up out er dat grave. I see him an' he look jest as natu'al as he done 'fore dey bury him. An' he look satisfy, an' he look like he taken a great interest in

Bur Rabbit an' de little beasts an' birds. An' he set down on de top er he own grave, an' carry on a long compersation wid all dem animals. An' dem owl look like dey never was guh git through. You know dem ole owl—de ole folks always is say dey is dead folks.

But dat ain' all. Atter dey done wored dey self out wid compersation, I see Bur Rabbit take he fiddle an' put it under he chin an' start to playin'. An' while I watch, I see Bur Rabbit step back on de grave an' Simon were gone.

FREDERICK DOUGLASS

Frederick Douglass was the first to give the circle a double meaning. Associated with his slave past, it signified for Douglass the confinements of bondage and enforced ignorance. And yet it also stood for community, as it always had—for the friends and family he had left behind when he escaped to the North. Outside of the circle of slavery, Douglass understood things he could not understand when he was still within it, but the cost of such understanding was exile and tears. This paradox, so beautifully expressed in the following paragraphs from Douglass's 1845 Narrative of the Life of Frederick Douglass, an American Slave, Written by Himself, *lies at the heart of the circle as we find it drawn in African-American writing.*

THE CIRCLE OF SLAVERY

The slaves selected to go to the Great House Farm, for the monthly allowance for themselves and their fellow-slaves, were peculiarly enthusiastic. While on their way, they would make the dense old woods, for miles around, reverberate with their wild songs, revealing at once the highest joy and the deepest sadness. They would compose and sing as they went along, consulting neither time nor tune. The thought that came up, came out—if not in the word, in the sound;—and as frequently in the one as in the other. They would sometimes sing the most pathetic sentiment in the most rapturous tone, and the most rapturous sentiment in the most pathetic tone. Into all of their songs they would manage to weave something of the Great House Farm. Especially would they do this, when leaving home. They would then sing most exultingly the following words:—

> "I am going away to
> the Great House Farm!
> O, yea! O, yea! O!"

This they would sing, as a chorus, to words which to many would seem unmeaning jargon, but which, nevertheless, were full of meaning to themselves. I have sometimes thought that the mere hearing of those songs would do more to impress some minds with the horrible character of slavery, than the reading of whole volumes of philosophy on the subject could do.

I did not, when a slave, understand the deep meaning of those rude and apparently incoherent songs. I was myself within the circle; so that I neither saw nor heard as those without might see and hear. They told a tale of woe which was then altogether beyond my feeble comprehension; they were tones loud, long, and deep; they breathed the prayer and complaint of souls boiling over with the bitterest anguish. Every tone was a testimony against slavery, and a prayer to God for deliverance from chains. The hearing of those wild notes always depressed my spirit, and filled me with ineffable sadness. I have frequently found myself in tears while hearing them. The mere recurrence to those songs, even now, afflicts me; and while I am writing these lines, an expression of feeling has already found its way down my cheek. To those songs I trace my first glimmering conception of the dehumanizing character of slavery. I can never get rid of that conception. Those songs still follow me, to deepen my hatred of slavery.

HARRIET JACOBS

Harriet Jacobs escaped slavery, not by leaving the circle but by hiding deep within it. Terrified by the sexual advances of her master, Dr. Flint, Jacobs hid for seven years in a crawl-space beneath the roof of her free grandmother's house. From there she watched her enslaved son and daughter grow up. Later, she escaped to the North, worked for the abolition of slavery, and in 1861 published the story of her life, Incidents in the Life of a Slave Girl. *She knew Frederick Douglass and admired his work. Perhaps she had his circle in mind when she called her old hideaway "the loophole of retreat." Here she recalls her first days in the tiny space.*

THE LOOPHOLE OF RETREAT

To this hole I was conveyed as soon as I entered the house. The air was stifling; the darkness total. A bed had been spread on the floor. I could sleep quite comfortably on one side; but the slope was so sudden that I could not turn on the other without hitting the roof. The rats and mice ran over my bed; but I was weary, and I slept such sleep as the wretched may, when a tempest has passed over them. Morning came. I knew it only by the noises I heard; for in my small den day and night were all the same. I suffered for air even more than for light. But I was not comfortless. I heard the voices of my children. There was joy and there was sadness in the sound. It made my tears flow. How I longed to speak to them! I was eager to look on their faces; but there was no hole, no crack, through which I could peep. This continued darkness was oppressive. It seemed horrible to sit or lie in a cramped position day after day, without one gleam of light. Yet I would have chosen this, rather than my lot as a slave, though white people considered it an easy one; and it was so compared with the fate of others. I was never cruelly overworked; I was never lacerated with the whip from head to foot; I was never so beaten and bruised that I could not turn from one side to the other; I never had my heel-strings cut to prevent my running away; I was never chained to a log and forced to drag it about, while I toiled in the fields from morning till night; I was never branded with hot iron, or torn by bloodhounds. On the contrary, I had always been kindly treated, and tenderly cared for, until I came into the hands of Dr. Flint. I had never wished for freedom till then. But though my life in slavery was comparatively devoid of hardships, God pity the woman who is compelled to lead such a life!

My food was passed up to me through the trap-door my uncle had contrived; and my grandmother, my uncle Phillip, and aunt Nancy would seize such opportunities as they could, to mount up there and chat with me at the opening.

But of course this was not safe in the daytime. It must all be done in darkness. It was impossible for me to move in an erect position, but I crawled about my den for exercise. One day I hit my head against something, and found it was a gimlet [a tool for boring holes]. My uncle had left it sticking there when he made the trap-door. I was as rejoiced as Robinson Crusoe could have been at finding such a treasure. It put a lucky thought into my head. I said to myself, "Now I will have some light. Now I will see my children." I did not dare to begin my work during the daytime, for fear of attracting attention. But I groped round; and having found the side next the street, where I could frequently see my children, I stuck the gimlet in and waited for evening. I bored three rows of holes, one above another; then I bored out the interstices between. I thus succeeded in making one hole about an inch long and an inch broad. I sat by it till late into the night, to enjoy the little whiff of air that floated in. In the morning I watched for my children. The first person I saw in the street was Dr. Flint. I had a shuddering, superstitious feeling that it was a bad omen. Several familiar faces passed by. At last I heard the merry laugh of children, and presently two sweet little faces were looking up at me, as though they knew I was there, and were conscious of the joy they imparted. How I longed to *tell* them I was there!

PAUL LAURENCE DUNBAR

Born in 1872 to former slaves, Paul Laurence Dunbar honored his parents' language and experience in many of his poems, including "An Ante-Bellum Sermon," from his 1896 Lyrics of Lowly Life. *The poem's speaker is an enslaved preacher, and in the opening lines he has gathered around him a circle of fellow slaves for "some words of comfo't." The subject of his stirring sermon is God's deliverance of Moses and the Israelites from bondage. He knows that he is "preachin' discontent," and his fear that others will think so too reminds us that this circle of listeners is drawn in a "howlin' wildaness" of hostile slaveholders.*

AN ANTE-BELLUM SERMON

We is gathahed hyeah, my brothahs,
    In dis howlin' wildaness,
Fu' to speak some words of comfo't
    To each othah in distress.
An' we chooses fu' ouah subjic'
    Dis—we'll 'splain it by an' by;
      "An' de Lawd said, 'Moses, Moses,'
    An' de man said, 'Hyeah am I.' "

Now ole Pher'oh, down in Egypt,
    Was de wuss man evah bo'n,
An' he had de Hebrew chillun
    Down dah wukin' in his co'n;
'Twell de Lawd got tiahed o' his foolin',
    An' sez he: "I'll let him know—
Look hyeah, Moses, go tell Pher'oh
    Fu' to let dem chillun go."

"An' ef he refuse to do it,
    I will make him rue de houah,
Fu' I'll empty down on Egypt
    All de vials of my powah."

Yes, he did—an' Pher'oh's ahmy
    Wasn't wuth a ha'f a dime;
Fu' de Lawd will he'p his chillun,
    You kin trust him evah time.

An' yo' enemies may 'sail you
    In de back an' in de front;
But de Lawd is all aroun' you,
    Fu' to ba' de battle's brunt.
Dey kin fo'ge yo' chains an' shackles
    F'om de mountains to de sea;
But de Lawd will sen' some Moses
    Fu' to set his chillun free.

An' de lan' shall hyeah his thundah,
    Lak a blas' f'om Gab'el's ho'n,
Fu' de Lawd of hosts is mighty
    When he girds his ahmor on.
But fu' feah some one mistakes me,
    I will pause right hyeah to say,
Dat I'm still a-preachin' ancient,
    I ain't talkin' 'bout to-day.

But I tell you, fellah christuns,
    Things'll happen mighty strange;
Now, de Lawd done dis fu' Isrul,
    An' his ways don't nevah change,
An' de love he showed to Isrul
    Wasn't all on Isrul spent;
Now don't run an' tell yo' mastahs
    Dat I's preachin' discontent.

Preaching with Circle, by Bill Traylor.

'Cause I isn't; I'se a-judgin'
  Bible people by deir ac's;
I'se a-givin' you de Scriptuah,
  I'se a-handin' you de fac's.
Cose ole Pher'oh b'lieved in slav'ry,
  But de Lawd he let him see,
Dat de people he put bref in,—
  Evah mothah's son was free.

An' dah's othahs thinks lak Pher'oh,
  But dey calls de Scriptuah liar,
Fu' de Bible says "a servant
  Is a-worthy of his hire."
An' you cain't git roun' nor thoo dat,
  An' you cain't git ovah it,
Fu' whatevah place you git in,
  Dis hyeah Bible too'll fit.

So you see de Lawd's intention,
  Evah sence de worl' began,
Was dat His almighty freedom
  Should belong to evah man,
But I think it would be bettah,
  Ef I'd pause agin to say,
Dat I'm talkin' 'bout ouah freedom
  In a Bibleistic way.

But de Moses is a-comin',
  An' he's comin', suah and fas'
We kin hyeah his feet a-trompin',
  We kin hyeah his trumpit blas'.
But I want to wa'n you people,

Don't you git too brigity;
An' don't you git to braggin'
'Bout dese things, you wait an' see.

But when Moses wif his powah
Comes an' sets us chillun free,
We will praise de gracious Mastah
Dat has gin us liberty;
An' we'll shout ouah halleluyahs,
On dat mighty reck'nin' day,
When we'se reco'nised ez citiz'—
Huh uh! Chillun, let us pray!

JAMES BALDWIN

Born in New York City to parents who had come north, James Baldwin first learned from them about racial violence and lynching in the Jim Crow South. This was the history that lay just beneath the surface for many African Americans in the North. In his 1948 short story "Sonny's Blues," Baldwin's unnamed narrator, an algebra teacher in Harlem, remembers the Sundays of his childhood when he learned this history in the family circle, a circle that is redrawn for him whenever he thinks of his mother.

THE FAMILY CIRCLE

The way I always see her is the way she used to be on a Sunday afternoon, say, when the old folks were talking after the big Sunday dinner. I always see her wearing pale blue. She'd be sitting on the sofa. And my father would be sitting in the easy chair, not far from her. And the living room would be full of church folks and relatives. There they sit, in chairs all around the living room, and the night is creeping up outside, but nobody knows it yet. You can see the darkness growing against the windowpanes and you hear the street noises every now and again, or maybe the jangling beat of a tambourine from one of the churches close by, but it's real quiet in the room. For a moment nobody's talking, but every face looks darkening, like the sky outside. And my mother rocks a little from the waist, and my father's eyes are closed. Everyone is looking at something a child can't see. For a minute they've forgotten the children. Maybe a kid is lying on the rug, half asleep. Maybe somebody's got a kid in his lap and is absent-mindedly stroking the kid's head. Maybe there's a kid, quiet and big-eyed, curled up in a big chair in the corner. The silence, the darkness coming, and the darkness in the faces frighten the child obscurely. He hopes that the hand which strokes his forehead will never stop—will never die. He hopes that there will never come a time when the old folks won't be sitting around the living room, talking about where they've come from, and what they've seen, and what's happened to them and their kinfolk.

But something deep and watchful in the child knows that this is bound to end, is already ending. In a moment someone will get up and turn on the light. Then the old folks will remember the children and they won't talk any more that day. And when light fills the room, the child is filled with darkness. He knows that every time this happens he's moved just a little closer to that darkness outside. The darkness outside is what the old folks have been talking about. It's what they've come from. It's what they endure. The child knows that they won't talk any more because if he knows too much about what's happened to *them*, he'll know too much too soon, about what's going to happen to *him*.

TONI MORRISON

In this scene from her 1987 novel Beloved, *Nobel Laureate Toni Morrison offers another version of the sacred circle. On warm Saturday afternoons, Baby Suggs, once a slave, gathers her neighbors around her to hear the story of their own abused and perishing flesh. As in Dunbar's "An Ante Bellum Sermon," the circle thus drawn is a visible emblem of the community within which African Americans find guidance, protection, and nurture.*

BABY SUGGS IN THE CLEARING

When warm weather came, Baby Suggs, holy, followed by every black man, woman and child who could make it through, took her great heart to the Clearing—a wide-open place cut deep in the woods nobody knew for what at the end of a path known only to deer and whoever cleared the land in the first place. In the heat of every Saturday afternoon, she sat in the clearing while the people waited among the trees.

After situating herself on a huge flat-sided rock, Baby Suggs bowed her head and prayed silently. The company watched her from the trees. They knew she was ready when she put her stick down. Then she shouted, "Let the children come!" and they ran from the trees toward her. "Let your mothers hear you laugh," she told them, and the woods rang. The adults looked on and could not help smiling.

Then "Let the grown men come," she shouted. They stepped out one by one from among the ringing trees.

"Let your wives and your children see you dance," she told them, and groundlife shuddered under their feet.

Finally she called the women to her. "Cry," she told them. "For the living and the dead. Just cry." And without covering their eyes the women let loose.

It started that way: laughing children, dancing men, crying women and then it got mixed up. Women stopped crying and danced; men sat down and cried; children danced, women laughed, children cried until, exhausted and riven, all and each lay about the Clearing damp and gasping for breath. In the silence that followed, Baby Suggs, holy, offered up to them her great big heart.

She did not tell them to clean up their lives or to go and sin no more. She did not tell them they were the blessed of the earth, its inheriting meek or its glorybound pure.

She told them that the only grace they could have was the grace they could imagine. That if they could not see it, they would not have it.

"Here," she said, "in this here place, we flesh; flesh that weeps, laughs; flesh that dances on bare feet in grass. Love it. Love it hard. Yonder they do not love your flesh. They despise it. They don't love your eyes; they'd just as soon pick em out. No more do they love the skin on your back. Yonder they flay it. And O my people they do not love your hands. Those they only use, tie, bind, chop off and leave empty. Love your hands! Love them. Raise them up and kiss them. Touch others with them, pat them together, stroke them on your face 'cause they don't love that either. *You* got to love it, *you!* And no, they ain't in love with your mouth. Yonder, out there, they will see it broken and break it again. What you say out of it they will not heed. What you scream from it they do not hear. What you put into it to nourish your body they will snatch away and give you leavins instead. No, they don't love your mouth. *You* got to love it. This is flesh I'm talking about here. Flesh that needs to be loved.

RITA DOVE

This recent poem by Poet Laureate Rita Dove seems to recall both Bur Rabbit and Frederick Douglass. Like Bur Rabbit, the musician's grandfather could charm the small animals into a circle with his playing, and when he died they kept his music going for two days. This evidence of the sacred circle may have frightened the musician into leaving the South, as the last line suggests, but he too keeps the music going, bringing it with him to Philadelphia. From there, like Douglass, who fled the circle of slavery, he looks back in wonder and affection at his own and his people's past.

THE MUSICIAN TALKS ABOUT 'PROCESS'
(after Anthony "Spoons" Pough)

> I learned the spoons from
> my grandfather, who was blind.
> Every day he'd go into the woods
> 'cause that was his thing.
> He met all kinds of creatures,
> birds and squirrels,
> and while he was feeding them
> he'd play the spoons,

and after they finished
they'd stay and listen.

When I go into Philly
on a Saturday night,
I don't need nothing but
my spoons and the music.
Laid out on my knees
they look so quiet,
but when I pick them up
I can play to anything:
a dripping faucet,
a tambourine,
fish shining in a creek.

A funny thing:
when my grandfather died,
every creature sang.
And when the men went out
to get him, they kept singing.
They sung for two days,
all the birds, all the animals.
That's when I left the south.

DARRYL PINCKNEY

In the work of writer Darryl Pinckney, the sacred circle is drawn in surprising places, in the various cafeterias of school and work. The following paragraphs, from Pinckney's 1992 novel High Cotton, *remind us that the circle, though confining, is a place of mutual obligation and love.*

THE BLACK TABLE

A job couldn't be just a job, a source of "chump change" that passed for income, at least not for very long. Heritage had a way of catching up with you in the office cafeteria. It tapped you on the shoulder and made you feel bad about the thoughtlessness of your desires and actions. It made you feel as bad as when you didn't get up to give your seat to an old-timer, or when you ran ahead to the playground and forced the babysitter with the rheumatoid hip to try to keep up. I found myself looking around for a black table in the office cafeteria.

I had always courted the quick signals that said you were tolerated, put up with. The blacks at the cafeteria tables in high school, in college, handed back your solidarity, as if they were returning your bug collection, which was mostly paraffin anyway. One try, and after that you didn't have to ask how was metal shop class, how were the med boards going, how was the family, and they didn't have to waste their time saying fine, fine, and fine all afternoon, scratching purple knit caps, the emblems of fraternity, wondering what you were trying to prove, what had come over you.

If for some reason you didn't feel comfortable among them, that was your problem, but their body language said don't turn around and put yourself through changes and come on all friendly like a black alderman out for the vote. They knew your heart was in the right place, because your heart didn't belong to you. They kept it in a vault someplace, like an indiscreet letter or a forged bill of exchange in an old-fashioned blackmail scheme. Where your head was at was another story, but they'd vote for you anyway, because there was no one else to vote for.

All of this was communicated to me by the way six black men in the office cafeteria blinked and made room for my tray. Guilt is a wonderfully stimulating condition, like certain forms of incarceration. They said they were from maintenance, Xerox, mail services, production; carried themselves with an air that said they had been through battles, shared a common bond, that I couldn't just walk in and be part of it. I chose to be reminded of the army films at the beautiful drive-in during which as a child I had fallen asleep. In the unit there was always one who was vehemently detached. By the time I woke and the canopy of stars had thickened the loner had put his life on the line for the squad.

ANDREA LEE

In Andrea Lee's chapter "New African," from her 1984 novel Sarah Phillips, *the sacred circle in all of its meanings is especially vivid. The narrator refuses to join it as a child, fearful of losing her identity in the past, here represented by Aunt Bessie and her "old southern attitudes." She discovers its meaning only as an adult, after her father has died.*

NEW AFRICAN

On a hot Sunday morning in the summer of 1963, I was sitting restlessly with my mother, my brother Matthew, and my aunts Lily, Emma, and May in a central pew of the New African Baptist Church. It was mid-August, and the hum of the big electric fans at the back of the church was almost enough to muffle my father's voice from the pulpit; behind me I could hear Mrs. Gordon, a stout, feeble old woman who always complained of dizziness, remark sharply to her daughter that at the rate the air-conditioning fund was growing, it might as well be for the next century. Facing the congregation, my father—who was Reverend Phillips to the rest of the world—seemed hot himself; he mopped his brow with a handkerchief and drank several glasses of ice water from the heavy pitcher on the table by the pulpit. I looked at him critically. He's still reading the text, I thought. Then he'll do the sermon, then the baptism, and it will be an hour, maybe two.

I rubbed my chin and then idly began to snap the elastic band that held my red straw hat in place. What I would really like to do, I decided, would be to go home, put on my shorts, and climb up into the tree house I had set up the day before with Matthew. We'd nailed an old bushel basket up in the branches of the big maple that stretched above the sidewalk in front of the house; it made a sort of crow's nest where you could sit comfortably, except for a few splinters, and read, or peer through the dusty leaves at the cars that passed down the quiet suburban road. There was shade and wind and a feeling of high adventure up in the treetop, where the air seemed to vibrate with the dry rhythms of the cicadas; it was as different as possible from church, where the packed congregation sat in a near-visible miasma of emotion and cologne, and trolleys passing in the city street outside set the stained-glass windows rattling.

I slouched between Mama and Aunt Lily and felt myself going limp with lassitude and boredom, as if the heat had melted my bones; the only thing about me with any character seemed to be my firmly starched eyelet dress. Below the scalloped hem, my legs were skinny and wiry, the legs of a ten-year-old amazon, scarred from violent adventures with bicycles and skates. A fingernail tapped my wrist; it was Aunt Emma, reaching across Aunt Lily to press a piece of butterscotch into my hand. When I slipped the candy into my mouth, it tasted faintly of Arpège; my mother and her three sisters were monumental women, ample of bust and slim of ankle, with a weakness for elegant footwear and French perfume. As they leaned back and forth to exchange discreet tidbits of gossip, they fanned themselves and me with fans from the Byron J. Wiggins Funeral Parlor. The fans, which were fluttering throughout the church, bore a depiction of the Good Shepherd: a hollow-eyed blond Christ holding three fat pink-cheeked children. This Christ resembled the Christ who stood among apostles on the stained-glass windows of the church. Deacon Wiggins, a thoughtful man, had also provided New African with a few dozen fans bearing the picture of a black child praying, but I rarely saw those in use.

There was little that was new or very African about the New African Baptist Church. The original congregation had been formed in 1813 by three young men from Philadelphia's large community of free blacks, and before many generations had passed, it had become spiritual home to a collection of prosperous, conservative, generally light-skinned parishioners. The church was a gray Gothic structure, set on the corner of a run-down street in South Philadelphia a dozen blocks below Rittenhouse Square and a few blocks west of the spare, clannish Italian neighborhoods that produced Frankie Avalon and Frank Rizzo. At the turn of the century, the neighborhood had been a tidy collection of brick houses with scrubbed marble steps—the homes of a group of solid citizens whom Booker T. Washington, in a centennial address to the church, described as "the ablest Negro businessmen of our generation." Here my father had grown up aspiring to preach to the congregation of New African—an ambition encouraged by my grandmother Phillips, a formidable churchwoman. Here, too, my mother and her sisters had walked with linked arms to Sunday services, exchanging affected little catchphrases of French and Latin they had learned at Girls' High.

In the 1950s many of the parishioners, seized by the national urge toward the suburbs, moved to newly integrated towns outside the city, leaving the streets around New African to fill with bottles and papers and loungers. The big church stood suddenly isolated. It had not been abandoned—on Sundays the front steps overflowed with members who had driven in—but there was a tentative feeling in the atmosphere of those Sunday mornings, as if through the muddle of social change, the future of New African had become unclear. Matthew and I, suburban children, felt a mixture of pride and animosity toward the church. On the one hand, it was a marvelous private domain, a richly decorated and infinitely suggestive playground where we were petted by a congregation that adored our father; on the other hand, it seemed a bit like a dreadful old relative in the city, one who forced us into tedious visits and who linked us to a past that came to seem embarrassingly primitive as we grew older.

I slid down in my seat, let my head roll back, and looked

up at the blue arches of the church ceiling. Lower than these, in back of the altar, was an enormous gilded cross. Still lower, in a semicircle near the pulpit, sat the choir, flanked by two tall golden files of organ pipes, and below the choir was a somber crescent of dark-suited deacons. In front, at the center of everything, his bald head gleaming under the lights, was Daddy. On summer Sundays he wore white robes, and when he raised his arms, the heavy material fell in curving folds like the ridged petals of an Easter lily. Usually when I came through the crowd to kiss him after the service, his cheek against my lips felt wet and gravelly with sweat and a new growth of beard sprouted since morning. Today, however, was a baptismal Sunday, and I wouldn't have a chance to kiss him until he was freshly shaven and cool from the shower he took after the ceremony. The baptismal pool was in an alcove to the left of the altar; it had mirrored walls and red velvet curtains, and above it, swaying on a string, hung a stuffed white dove.

Daddy paused in the invocation and asked the congregation to pray. The choir began to sing softly:

> Blessed assurance,
> Jesus is mine!
> Oh what a foretaste
> Of glory divine!

In the middle of the hymn, I edged my head around my mother's cool, muscular arm (she swam every day of the summer) and peered at Matthew. He was sitting bolt upright holding a hymnal and a pencil, his long legs inside his navy-blue summer suit planted neatly in front of him, his freckled thirteen-year-old face that was so like my father's wearing not the demonic grin it bore when we played alone but a maddeningly composed, attentive expression. "Two hours!" I mouthed at him, and pulled back at a warning pressure from my mother. Then I joined in the singing, feeling disappointed: Matthew had returned me a glance of scorn. Just lately he had started acting very superior and tolerant about tedious Sunday mornings. A month before, he'd been baptized, marching up to the pool in a line of white-robed children as the congregation murmured happily about Reverend Phillips's son. Afterward Mrs. Pinkston, a tiny, yellow-skinned old woman with a blind left eye, had come up to me and given me a painful hug, whispering that she was praying night and day for the pastor's daughter to hear the call as well.

I bit my fingernails whenever I thought about baptism; the subject brought out a deep-rooted balkiness in me. Ever since I could remember, Matthew and I had made a game of dispelling the mysteries of worship with a gleeful secular eye: we knew how the bread and wine were prepared for Communion, and where Daddy bought his robes (Ekhardt Brothers, in North Philadelphia, makers also of robes for choirs, academicians, and judges). Yet there was an un-assailable magic about an act as public and dramatic as baptism. I felt toward it the slightly exasperated awe a stage-hand might feel on realizing that although he can identify with professional exactitude the minutest components of a show, there is still something indefinable in the power that makes it a cohesive whole. Though I could not have put it into words, I believed that the decision to make a frightening

and embarrassing backward plunge into a pool of sanctified
water meant that one had received a summons to Christianity as unmistakable as the blare of an automobile horn. I
believed this with the same fervor with which, already, I
believed in the power of romance, especially in the miraculous efficacy of a lover's first kiss. I had never been kissed by
a lover, nor had I heard the call to baptism.

For a Baptist minister and his wife, my father and mother
were unusually relaxed about religion; Matthew and I had
never been required to read the Bible, and my father's sermons had been criticized by some older church members
for omitting the word "sin." Mama and Daddy never tried to
push me toward baptism, but a number of other people did.
Often on holidays, when I had retreated from the noise of
the family dinner table and sat trying to read in my favorite
place (the window seat in Matthew's room, with the curtains
drawn to form a tent), Aunt Lily would come and find me.
Aunt Lily was the youngest of my mother's sisters, a kinder-
garten teacher with the fatally overdeveloped air of quaint-
ness that is the infallible mark of an old maid. Aunt Lily
hoped and hoped again with various suitors, but even I
knew she would never find a husband. I respected her
because she gave me wonderful books of fairy tales, in-
scribed in her neat, loopy hand; when she talked about
religion, however, she assumed an anxious, flirtatious air
that made me cringe. "Well, Miss Sarah, what are you scared
of?" she would ask, tugging gently on one of my braids and
bringing her plump face so close to mine that I could see her
powder, which was, in accordance with the custom of fashionable colored ladies, several shades lighter than her olive

skin. "God isn't anyone to be afraid of!" she'd continue as I looked at her with my best deadpan expression. "He's someone nice, just as nice as your daddy"—I had always suspected Aunt Lily of having a crush on my father—"and he loves you, in the same way your daddy does!"

"You would make us all so happy!" I was told at different times by Aunt Lily, Aunt Emma, and Aunt May. The only people who said nothing at all were Mama and Daddy, but I sensed in them a thoughtful, suppressed wistfulness that maddened me.

After the hymn, Daddy read aloud a few verses from the third chapter of Luke, verses I recognized in the almost instinctive way in which I was familiar with all of the well-traveled parts of the Old and New Testaments. "Prepare the way of the Lord, make his paths straight," read my father in a mild voice. "Every valley shall be filled, and every mountain and hill shall be brought low, and the crooked shall be made straight, and the rough paths made smooth, and all flesh shall see the salvation of God."

He had a habit of pausing to fix his gaze on part of the congregation as he read, and that Sunday he seemed to be talking to a small group of strangers who sat in the front row. These visitors were young white men and women, students from Philadelphia colleges, who for the past year had been coming to hear him talk. It was hard to tell them apart: all the men seemed to have beards, and the women wore their hair long and straight. Their informal clothes stood out in that elaborate assembly, and church members whispered angrily that the young women didn't wear hats. I found the students appealing and rather romantic, with their earnest eyes and timid air of being perpetually sorry about something. It was clear that they had good intentions, and I couldn't understand why so many of the adults in the congregation seemed to dislike them so much. After services, they would hover around Daddy. "Never a more beautiful civil rights sermon!" they would say in low, fervent voices. Sometimes they seemed to have tears in their eyes.

I wasn't impressed by their praise of my father; it was only what everyone said. People called him a champion of civil rights; he gave speeches on the radio, and occasionally he appeared on television. (The first time I'd seen him on Channel 5, I'd been gravely disappointed by the way he looked: the bright lights exaggerated the furrows that ran between his nose and mouth, and his narrow eyes gave him a sinister air; he looked like an Oriental villain in a Saturday afternoon thriller.) During the past year he had organized a boycott that integrated the staff of a huge frozen-food plant in Philadelphia, and he'd been away several times to attend marches and meetings in the South. I was privately embarrassed to have a parent who freely admitted going to jail in Alabama, but the students who visited New African seemed to think it almost miraculous. Their conversations with my father were peppered with references to places I had never seen, towns I imagined as being swathed in a mist of darkness visible: Selma, Macon, Birmingham, Biloxi.

Matthew and I had long ago observed that what Daddy generally did in his sermons was to speak very softly and then surprise everyone with a shout. Of course, I knew that there was more to it than that; even in those days I recognized a genius of personality in my father. He loved crowds, handling them with the expert good humor of a man entirely in his element. At church banquets, at the vast annual picnic that was held beside a lake in New Jersey, or at any gathering in the backyards and living rooms of the town where we lived, the sound I heard most often was the booming of my father's voice followed by shouts of laughter from the people around him. He had a passion for oratory; at home, he infuriated Matthew and me by staging absurd debates at the dinner table, verbal melees that he won quite selfishly, with a loud crow of delight at his own virtuosity. "Is a fruit a vegetable?" he would demand. "Is a zipper a machine?" Matthew and I would plead with him to be quiet as we strained to get our own points across, but it was no use. When the last word had resounded and we sat looking at him in irritated silence, he would clear his throat, settle his collar, and resume eating, his face still glowing with an irrepressible glee.

When he preached, he showed the same private delight. A look of rapt pleasure seemed to broaden and brighten the contours of his angular face until it actually appeared to give off light as he spoke. He could preach in two very different ways. One was the delicate, sonorous idiom of formal oratory, with which he must have won the prizes he held from his seminary days. The second was a hectoring, insinuating, incantatory tone, full of the rhythms of the South he had never lived in, linking him to generations of thunderous Baptist preachers. When he used this tone, as he was doing now, affectionate laughter rippled through the pews.

"I know," he said, looking out over the congregation and blinking his eyes rapidly, "that there are certain people in

Aspects of Negro Life: From Slavery through Reconstruction, by Aaron Douglas. This mural is part of a series depicting the history of black Americans.

this room—oh, I don't have to name names or point a finger—who have ignored that small true voice, the voice that is the voice of Jesus calling out in the shadowy depths of the soul. And while you all are looking around and wondering just who those 'certain people' are, I want to tell you all a secret: they are you and me, and your brother-in-law, and

every man, woman, and child in this room this morning. All
of us listen to our bellies when they tell us it is time to eat, we
pay attention to our eyes when they grow heavy from want-
ing sleep, but when it comes to the sacred knowledge our
hearts can offer, we are deaf, dumb, blind, and senseless.
Throw away that blindness, that deafness, that sulky indif-

ference. When all the world lies to you, Jesus will tell you what is right. Listen to him. Call on him. In these times of confusion, when there are a dozen different ways to turn, and Mama and Papa can't help you, trust Jesus to set you straight. Listen to him. The Son of God has the answers. Call on him. Call on him. Call on him."

The sermon was punctuated with an occasional loud "Amen!" from Miss Middleton, an excitable old lady whose eyes flashed defiantly at the reproving faces of those around her. New African was not the kind of Baptist church where shouting was a normal part of the service; I occasionally heard my father mock the staid congregation by calling it Saint African. Whenever Miss Middleton loosed her tongue (sometimes she went off into fits of rapturous shrieks and had to be helped out of the service by the church nurse), my mother and aunts exchanged grimaces and shrugged, as if confronted by incomprehensibly barbarous behavior.

When Daddy had spoken the final words of the sermon, he drank a glass of water and vanished through a set of red velvet curtains to the right of the altar. At the same time, the choir began to sing what was described in the church bulletin as a "selection." These selections were always arenas for the running dispute between the choirmaster and the choir. Jordan Grimes, the choirmaster, was a Curtis graduate who was partial to Handel, but the choir preferred artistic spirituals performed in the lush, heroic style of Paul Robeson. Grimes had triumphed that Sunday. As the choir gave a spirited but unwilling rendition of Agnus Dei, I watched old Deacon West smile in approval. A Spanish-American War veteran, he admitted to being ninety-four but was said to be older; his round yellowish face, otherwise unwrinkled, bore three deep, deliberate-looking horizontal creases on the brow, like carvings on a scarab. "That old man is as flirtatious as a boy of twenty!" my mother often said, watching his stiff, courtly movements among the ladies of the church. Sometimes he gave me a dry kiss and a piece of peppermint candy after the service; I liked his crackling white collars and smell of bay rum.

The selection ended; Jordan Grimes struck two deep chords on the organ, and the lights in the church went low. A subtle stir ran through the congregation, and I moved closer to my mother. This was the moment that fascinated and disturbed me more than anything else at church: the prelude to the ceremony of baptism. Deacon West rose and drew open the draperies that had been closed around the baptismal pool, and there stood my father in water to his waist. The choir began to sing:

> We're marching to Zion,
> Beautiful, beautiful Zion,
> We're marching upward to Zion,
> The beautiful city of God!

Down the aisle, guided by two church mothers, came a procession of eight children and adolescents. They wore white robes, the girls with white ribbons in their hair, and they all had solemn expressions of terror on their faces. I knew each one of them. There was Billy Price, a big, slow-moving boy of thirteen, the son of Deacon Price. There were the Duckery twins. There was Caroline Piggee, whom I hated because of her long, soft black curls, her dimpled pink face, and her lisp that ravished grown-ups. There was Georgie Battis and Sue Anne Ivory, and Wendell and Mabel Cullen.

My mother gave me a nudge. "Run up to the side of the pool!" she whispered. It was the custom of unbaptized children to watch the ceremony from the front of the church. They sat on the knees of the deacons and church mothers, and it was not unusual for a child to volunteer then and there for next month's baptism. I made my way quickly down the dark aisle, feeling the carpet slip under the smooth soles of my patent-leather shoes.

When I reached the side of the pool, I sat down in the bony lap of Bessie Gray, an old woman who often took care of Matthew and me when our parents were away; we called her Aunt Bessie. She was a fanatically devout Christian whose strict ideas on child-rearing had evolved over decades of domestic service to a rich white family in Delaware. The link between us, a mixture of hostility and grudging affection, had been forged in hours of pitched battles over bedtimes and proper behavior. Her worshipful respect for my father, whom she called "the Rev," was exceeded only by her pride—the malice-tinged pride of an omniscient family servant—in her "white children," to whom she often unflatteringly compared Matthew and me. It was easy to see why my mother and her circle of fashionable matrons described Bessie Gray as "archaic"—one had only to look at her black straw hat attached with three enormous old-fashioned pins to her knot of frizzy white hair. Her lean, brown-skinned face was dominated by a hawk nose inherited from some Indian ancestor and punctuated by a big black mole; her eyes were small, shrewd, and baleful. She talked in ways that were already passing into history and parody, and she wore a thick orange face powder that smelled like dead leaves.

I leaned against her spare bosom and watched the other children clustered near the pool, their bonnets and hair ribbons and round heads outlined in the dim light. For a minute it was very still. Somewhere in the hot, darkened church a baby gave a fretful murmur; from outside came the sound of cars passing in the street. The candidates for baptism, looking stiff and self-conscious, stood lined up on the short stairway leading to the pool. Sue Anne Ivory fiddled with her sleeve and then put her fingers in her mouth.

Daddy spoke the opening phrases of the ceremony: "In the Baptist Church, we do not baptize infants, but believe that a person must choose salvation for himself."

I didn't listen to the words; what I noticed was the music of the whole—how the big voice darkened and lightened in tone, and how the grand architecture of the Biblical sentences ennobled the voice. The story, of course, was about Jesus and John the Baptist. One phrase struck me newly each time: "This is my beloved son, in whom I am well pleased!" Daddy sang out these words in a clear, triumphant tone, and the choir echoed him. Ever since I could understand it, this phrase had made me feel melancholy; it seemed to expose a hard knot of disobedience that had always lain inside me. When I heard it, I thought enviously of Matthew, for whom life seemed to be a sedate and ordered affair: he, not I, was a child in whom a father could be well pleased.

Daddy beckoned to Billy Price, the first baptismal candidate in line, and Billy, ungainly in his white robe, descended the steps into the pool. In soft, slow voices the choir began to sing:

> Wade in the water,
> Wade in the water, children,
> Wade in the water,
> God gonna trouble
> The water.

In spite of Jordan Grimes's efforts, the choir swayed like a gospel chorus as it sang this spiritual; the result was to add an eerie jazz beat to the minor chords. The music gave me gooseflesh. Daddy had told me that this was the same song that the slaves had sung long ago in the South, when they gathered to be baptized in rivers and streams. Although I cared little about history, and found it hard to picture the slaves as being any ancestors of mine, I could clearly imagine them coming together beside a broad muddy river that wound away between trees drooping with strange vegetation. They walked silently in lines, their faces very black against their white clothes, leading their children. The whole scene was bathed in the heavy golden light that meant age and solemnity, the same light that seemed to weigh down the Israelites in illustrated volumes of Bible stories, and that shone now from the baptismal pool, giving the ceremony the air of a spectacle staged in a dream.

All attention in the darkened auditorium was now focused on the pool, where between the red curtains my father stood holding Billy Price by the shoulders. Daddy stared into

Billy's face, and the boy stared back, his lips set and trembling. "And now, by the power invested in me," said Daddy, "I baptize you in the name of the Father, the Son, and the Holy Ghost." As he pronounced these words, he conveyed a tenderness as efficient and impersonal as a physician's professional manner; beneath it, however, I could see a strong private gladness, the same delight that transformed his face when he preached a sermon. He paused to flick a drop of water off his forehead, and then, with a single smooth, powerful motion of his arms, he laid Billy Price back into the water as if he were putting an infant to bed. I caught my breath as the boy went backward. When he came up, sputtering, two church mothers helped him out of the pool and through a doorway into a room where he would be dried and dressed. Daddy shook the water from his hands and gave a slight smile as another child entered the pool.

One by one, the baptismal candidates descended the steps. Sue Anne Ivory began to cry and had to be comforted. Caroline Piggee blushed and looked up at my father with such a coquettish air that I jealously wondered how he could stand it. After a few baptisms my attention wandered, and I began to gnaw the edge of my thumb and to peer at the pale faces of the visiting college students. Then I thought about Matthew, who had punched me in the arm that morning and had shouted, "No punchbacks!" I thought as well about a collection of horse chestnuts I meant to assemble in the fall, and about two books, one whose subject was adults and divorces, and another, by E. Nesbit, that continued the adventures of the Bastable children.

After Wendell Cullen had left the water (glancing uneasily

back at the wet robe trailing behind him), Daddy stood alone among the curtains and the mirrors. The moving reflections from the pool made the stuffed dove hanging over him seem to flutter on its string. "Dear Lord," said Daddy, as Jordan Grimes struck a chord, "bless these children who have chosen to be baptized in accordance with your teaching, and who have been reborn to carry out your work. In each of them, surely, you are well pleased." He paused, staring out into the darkened auditorium. "And if there is anyone out there—man, woman, child—who wishes to be baptized next month, let him come forward now." He glanced around eagerly. "Oh, do come forward and give Christ your heart and give me your hand!"

Just then Aunt Bessie gave me a little shake and whispered sharply, "Go on up and accept Jesus!"

I stiffened and dug my bitten fingernails into my palms. The last clash of wills I had had with Aunt Bessie had been when she, crazily set in her old southern attitudes, had tried to make me wear an enormous straw hat, as her "white children" did, when I played outside in the sun. The old woman had driven me to madness, and I had ended up spanked and sullen, crouching moodily under the dining-room table. But this was different, outrageous, none of her business, I thought. I shook my head violently and she took advantage of the darkness of the church to seize both of my shoulders and jounce me with considerable roughness, whispering, "Now, listen, young lady! Your daddy up there is calling you to Christ. Your big brother has already offered his soul to the Lord. Now Daddy wants his little girl to step forward."

"No, he doesn't." I glanced at the baptismal pool, where my father was clasping the hand of a strange man who had come up to him. I hoped that this would distract Aunt Bessie, but she was tireless.

"Your mama and your aunt Lily and your aunt May all want you to answer the call. You're hurting them when you say no to Jesus."

"No, I'm not!" I spoke out loud and I saw the people nearby turn to look at me. At the sound of my voice, Daddy, who was a few yards away, faltered for a minute in what he was saying and glanced over in my direction.

Aunt Bessie seemed to lose her head. She stood up abruptly, pulling me with her, and, while I was still frozen in a dreadful paralysis, tried to drag me down the aisle toward my father. The two of us began a brief struggle that could not have lasted for more than a few seconds but that seemed an endless mortal conflict—my slippery patent-leather shoes braced against the floor, my straw hat sliding cockeyed and lodging against one ear, my right arm twisting and twisting in the iron circle of the old woman's grip, my nostrils full of the dead-leaf smell of her powder and black skirts. In an instant I had wrenched my arm free and darted up the aisle toward Mama, my aunts, and Matthew. As I slipped past the pews in the darkness, I imagined that I could feel eyes fixed on me and hear whispers. "What'd you do, dummy?" whispered Matthew, tugging on my sash as I reached our pew, but I pushed past him without answering. Although it was hot in the church, my teeth were chattering: it was the first time I had won a battle with a grownup, and the earth seemed to be about to cave in beneath me. I squeezed in between Mama and Aunt Lily just as the lights came back on in the church. In the baptismal pool, Daddy raised his arms for the last time. "The Lord bless you and keep you," came his big voice. "The Lord be gracious unto you, and give you peace."

What was curious was how uncannily subdued my parents were when they heard of my skirmish with Aunt Bessie. Normally they were swift to punish Matthew and me for misbehavior in church and for breaches in politeness toward adults; this episode combined the two, and smacked of sacrilege besides. Yet once I had made an unwilling apology to the old woman (as I kissed her she shot me such a vengeful glare that I realized that forever after it was to be war to the death between the two of us), I was permitted, once we had driven home, to climb up into the green shade of the big maple tree I had dreamed of throughout the service. In those days, more than now, I fell away into a remote dimension whenever I opened a book; that afternoon, as I sat with rings of sunlight and shadow moving over my arms and legs, and winged yellow seeds plopping down on the pages of *The Story of the Treasure Seekers*, I felt a vague uneasiness floating in the back of my mind—a sense of having misplaced something, of being myself misplaced. I was holding myself quite aloof from considering what had happened, as I did with most serious events, but through the adventures of the Bastables I kept remembering the way my father had looked when he'd heard what had happened. He hadn't looked severe or angry, but merely puzzled, and he had regarded me with the same puzzled expression, as if he'd just discovered that I existed and didn't know what to do with me. "What happened, Sairy?" he asked, using an old baby nickname, and I said, "I didn't want to go up there." I hadn't cried at all, and that was another curious thing.

After that Sunday, through some adjustment in the adult spheres beyond my perception, all pressure on me to accept baptism ceased. I turned twelve, fifteen, then eighteen without being baptized, a fact that scandalized some of the congregation; however, my parents, who openly discussed everything else, never said a word to me. The issue, and the episode that had illuminated it, was surrounded by a clear ring of silence that, for our garrulous family, was something close to supernatural. I continued to go to New African—in fact, continued after Matthew, who dropped out abruptly during his freshman year in college; the ambiguousness in my relations with the old church gave me at times an inflated sense of privilege (I saw myself as a romantically isolated religious heroine, a sort of self-made Baptist martyr) and at other times a feeling of loss that I was too proud ever to acknowledge. I never went up to take my father's hand, and he never commented upon that fact to me. It was an odd pact, one that I could never consider in the light of day; I stored it in the subchambers of my heart and mind. It was only much later, after he died, and I left New African forever, that I began to examine the peculiar gift of freedom my father—whose entire soul was in the church, and in his exuberant, bewitching tongue—had granted me through his silence.

THE VEIL:
W.E.B. DU BOIS
AND THE GEOMETRY
OF DISUNITY

And anyone can tell
You think you know me well,
But you don't know me.

—Popular ballad,
sung by Ray Charles

Frederick Douglass saw slavery as a confining circle to be escaped, whatever the cost. In 1903, forty years after the abolition of slavery, New England–born historian and philosopher W.E.B. Du Bois offered another image of the nation's racial practices in *The Souls of Black Folk*.

In the chapter entitled "Of Our Spiritual Strivings," Du Bois recounted that day in his boyhood when he first learned he was different from his white classmates. He cast about for a word to describe the sudden change that came over his life in that moment—a "shadow" fell, a "prison-house" closed round. More than anything, a "vast veil" descended between him and his white peers. To be black in America was, Du Bois concluded, to be "born with a veil."

It was a powerful idea, and one that continues to haunt—and to connect—the writings of African Americans. If the circle is the geometry of community, the veil is the geometry of disunity, a "color line" drawn between black and white Americans. Like the circle of slavery, the veil created a sense of solidarity and community, but it also excluded African Americans from the nation's wealth and progress. Du Bois's veil stood for all that continued to keep African Americans from prosperity and full citizenship in the American world, long after slavery had ended. In particular, it stood for Jim Crow segregation, the "separate but equal" doctrines and practices that made African Americans exiles in their own land.

Du Bois's veil had other meanings as well. The circle of slavery could be left behind, and indeed slavery itself could end. But the veil, like the horizon, was always there, no matter how far one went or how much time went by. Internal as well as external, it was a way of seeing, or not seeing, in a society divided by race. For African Americans it meant "second-sight" or "double consciousness," a troubling "gift" for seeing things from two points of view, one black and one white. For white Americans, too often it meant sheer blindness to any point of view but their own.

Du Bois's veil continues to suggest many things. As you read the selections in this chapter, you will see how often twentieth-century African-American writers have honored this language in shaping their contemporary experiences. Invoked by name or by one of its many meanings, Du Bois's veil has taken on an ancestral familiarity in the work of these and other writers. A profound symbol of disunity, it has brought a literary community into being.

Here are the paragraphs from his 1903 The Souls of Black Folk *in which W.E.B. Du Bois first wrote of the veil. Note how he works slowly toward his famous phrase and how he uses it to connect his own life to the lives of other African Americans. Bear in mind that the child "born with a veil"—or a portion of the mother's placenta still covering it—is regarded in many places as a good-luck child. Similarly, the seventh son of a seventh son is thought to possess second sight. These folk beliefs support Du Bois's thesis that the racial veil of African Americans is a blessing as well as a burden.*

THE VEIL

I remember well when the shadow swept across me. I was a little thing, away up in the hills of New England, where the dark Housatonic winds between Hoosac and Taghkanic to the sea. In a wee wooden schoolhouse, something put it into the boys' and girls' heads to buy gorgeous visiting-cards— ten cents a package—and exchange. The exchange was merry, till one girl, a tall newcomer, refused my card,— refused it peremptorily, with a glance. Then it dawned upon me with a certain suddenness that I was different from the others; or like, mayhap, in heart and life and longing, but shut out from their world by a vast veil. I had thereafter no desire to tear down that veil, to creep through; I held all beyond it in common contempt, and lived above it in a region of blue sky and great wandering shadows. That sky was bluest when I could beat my mates at examination-time, or beat them at a foot-race, or even beat their stringy heads. Alas, with the years all this fine contempt began to fade; for the worlds I longed for, and all their dazzling opportunities, were theirs, not mine. But they should not keep these prizes, I said; some, all, I would wrest from them. Just how I would do it I could never decide: by reading law, by healing the sick, by telling the wonderful tales that swam in my head,— some way. With other black boys the strife was not so fiercely sunny: their youth shrunk into tasteless sycophancy, or into silent hatred of the pale world about them and mocking distrust of everything white; or wasted itself in a bitter cry, Why did God make me an outcast and a stranger in mine own house? The shades of the prison-house closed round about us all: walls strait and stubborn to the whitest, but relentlessly narrow, tall, and unscalable to sons of night who must plod darkly on in resignation, or beat unavailing palms against the stone, or steadily, half hopelessly, watch the streak of blue above.

After the Egyptian and Indian, the Greek and Roman, the Teuton and Mongolian, the Negro is a sort of seventh son, born with a veil, and gifted with second-sight in this American world,—a world which yields him no true self-consciousness, but only lets him see himself through the revelation of the other world. It is a peculiar sensation, this double-consciousness, this sense of always looking at one's self through the eyes of others, of measuring one's soul by the tape of a world that looks on in amused contempt and pity. One ever feels his twoness,—an American, a Negro; two souls, two thoughts, two unreconciled strivings; two warring ideals in one dark body, whose dogged strength alone keeps it from being torn asunder.

RALPH ELLISON

Perhaps the most famous "take" on Du Bois's veil is Ralph Ellison's great 1952 novel Invisible Man. *In the book's opening paragraphs, Ellison's hero explains how the veil of race makes him invisible. As Du Bois's veil grants "second-sight" but prevents "true self-consciousness," so invisibility is both "advantageous" and "wearing on the nerves. . . . You often doubt if you really exist." But for Ellison's Invisible Man, there is no doubt that he is invisible because other people are blind.*

ON INVISIBILITY

I am an invisible man. No, I am not a spook like those who haunted Edgar Allan Poe; nor am I one of your Hollywood-movie ectoplasms. I am a man of substance, of flesh and bone, fiber and liquids—and I might even be said to possess a mind. I am invisible, understand, simply because people refuse to see me. Like the bodiless heads you see sometimes in circus sideshows, it is as though I have been surrounded by mirrors of hard, distorting glass. When they approach me they see only my surroundings, themselves, or figments of their imagination—indeed, everything and anything except me.

Nor is my invisibility exactly a matter of a bio-chemical accident to my epidermis. That invisibility to which I refer occurs because of a peculiar disposition of the eyes of those with whom I come in contact. A matter of the construction of their *inner* eyes, those eyes with which they look through their physical eyes upon reality. I am not complaining, nor

Tenement Window, by Ronald Joseph, 1939. *(Collection of Reba and Dave Williams)*

am I protesting either. It is sometimes advantageous to be unseen, although it is most often rather wearing on the nerves. Then too, you're constantly being bumped against by those of poor vision. Or again, you often doubt if you really exist. You wonder whether you aren't simply a phantom in other people's minds. Say, a figure in a nightmare which the sleeper tries with all his strength to destroy. It's when you feel like this that, out of resentment, you begin to bump people back. And, let me confess, you feel that way most of the time. You ache with the need to convince yourself that you do exist in the real world, that you're a part of all the sound and anguish, and you strike out with your fists, you curse and you swear to make them recognize you. And, alas, it's seldom successful.

One night I accidentally bumped into a man, and perhaps because of the near darkness he saw me and called me an insulting name. I sprang at him, seized his coat lapels and demanded that he apologize. He was a tall blond man, and as my face came close to his he looked insolently out of his blue eyes and cursed me, his breath hot in my face as he struggled. I pulled his chin down sharp upon the crown of my head, butting him as I had seen the West Indians do, and I felt his flesh tear and the blood gush out, and I yelled, "Apologize! Apologize!" But he continued to curse and struggle, and I butted him again and again until he went down heavily, on his knees, profusely bleeding. I kicked him repeatedly, in a frenzy because he still uttered insults though his lips were frothy with blood. Oh yes, I kicked him! And in my outrage I got out my knife and prepared to slit his throat, right there beneath the lamplight in the deserted street, holding him in the collar with one hand, and opening the knife with my teeth—when it occurred to me that the man had not *seen* me, actually; that he, as far as he knew, was in the midst of a walking nightmare! And I stopped the blade, slicing the air as I pushed him away, letting him fall back to the street. I stared at him hard as the lights of a car stabbed through the darkness. He lay there, moaning on the asphalt; a man almost killed by a phantom. It unnerved me. I was both disgusted and ashamed. I was like a drunken man myself, wavering about on weakened legs. Then I was amused: Something in this man's thick head had sprung out and beaten him within an inch of his life. I began to laugh at this crazy discovery. Would he have awakened at the point of death? Would Death himself have freed him for wakeful living? But I didn't linger. I ran away into the dark, laughing so hard I feared I might rupture myself. The next day I saw his picture in the *Daily News*, beneath a caption stating that he had been "mugged." Poor fool, poor blind fool, I thought with sincere compassion, mugged by an invisible man!

SAMUEL ALLEN

Du Bois's idea of "double-consciousness" is central to Samuel Allen's 1956 poem "A Moment Please," which shuffles together two seemingly different thoughts as if they were playing cards. The italicized lines speak dreamily of earth and time, while the alternate lines tell of a brutal encounter in the subway station. By the end, we understand the connection between this encounter and the speaker's sense that he is "the dupe of space, the toy of time."

A MOMENT PLEASE

When I gaze at the sun
          I walked to the subway booth
          for change for a dollar.
and know that this great earth
          Two adolescent girls stood there
          alive with eagerness to know
is but a fragment from it thrown
          all in their new found world
          there was for them to know
in heat and flame a billion years ago
          they looked at me and brightly asked
          "Are you Arabian?"
that then this world was lifeless
          I smiled and cautiously
          —for one grows cautious—
          shook my head.
as a billion hence,
          "Egyptian?"
it shall again be,
          Again I smiled and shook my head
          and walked away.
what moment is it that I am betrayed,
          I've gone but seven paces now
oppressed, cast down,
          and from behind comes swift the sneer
or warm with love or triumph?
          "Or Nigger?"

          A moment, please

What is it that to fury I am roused?
for still it takes a moment,
What meaning for me
now
is this unrested clan
. . . I turned
the dupe of space
and smiled
the toy of time?
and shook my head.

ERNEST GAINES

In the following paragraphs from his 1971 novel The Autobiography of Miss Jane Pittman, *Ernest Gaines invokes Du Bois's veil by name. Here, 108-year-old Miss Jane remembers Jimmy, a young activist who tried to involve her and her reluctant neighbors in a civil rights demonstration. Although she agreed to take part, Jane Pittman remembers sharing her neighbors' fears.*

THE BLACK VEIL

By the time he came to church Sunday the whole place had heard about it. Just Thomas was against even letting him come in the church, but Elder Banks told him nobody would ever be kept out of church long as he came there in peace. When Jimmy got up to talk some of the people went outside. Many of the ones who stayed didn't show interest or respect. I sat there looking at Jimmy, thinking: Jimmy, Jimmy, Jimmy, Jimmy, Jimmy. It's not that they don't love you, Jimmy; it's not that they don't want believe in you; but they don't know what you talking about. You talk of freedom, Jimmy. Freedom here is able to make a little living and have the white folks say you good. Black curtains hang at their windows, Jimmy: black quilts cover their body at night: a black veil cover their eyes, Jimmy; and the buzzing, buzzing, buzzing in their ears keep them from 'ciphering what you got to say. Oh, Jimmy, didn't they ask for you? And didn't He send you, and when they saw you, didn't they want you? They want you, Jimmy, but now you here they don't understand nothing you telling them. You see, Jimmy, they want you to cure the ache, but they want you to do it and don't give them pain. And the worse pain Jimmy, you can inflict is what you doing now—that's trying to make them see they good as the other man. You see, Jimmy, they been told from the cradle they wasn't—that they wasn't much better than the mule. You keep telling them this over and over, for hundreds and hundreds of years, they start thinking that way. The curtain, Jimmy, the quilt, the veil, the buzzing, buzzing, buzzing— two days, a few hours to clear all this away, Jimmy, is not enough time. How long will it take? How could I know? He works in mysterious ways; wonders to perform.

But look at me acting high and mighty. Don't the black curtain hang over my window; don't the veil cover my face?

CHARLES JOHNSON
Andrew, the narrator of Charles Johnson's Oxherding Tale, *is a runaway slave and recovering drug addict passing for white. His friend and mentor, Reb, is posing as his servant.*

The man hired to track them down is Horace Bannon, the Soulcatcher, who always gets his prey. In the following passage, these three men gather around a campfire to discuss the finer points of slave catching. Andrew's vision momentarily doubles as Bannon explains his technique, a technique that relies on a very particular reading of Du Bois's veil.

HORACE BANNON, SOULCATCHER

"There ain't many men what kin catch, or kill, a Negro the *right* way."

"There is," I ventured, "a right and wrong way to this?"

The Soulcatcher reached for his jug and poured three fingers of warm whiskey into his cup. Leaning back against the log, he rubbed his legs to start blood circulating again. A last rush of chandoo [opium] locked in my system, inactive until now, chose that moment to come to life, doubling my vision for an instant, twinning Bannon and the trees behind him. Time dissolved into a deeper silence, the universe breathing outward—a god's exhalation in sleep—then in, pointlessly. It was as though we were the last men in the world, survivors of a holocaust at Hegel's end of history, trying to figure out what went wrong. And then the Soulcatcher laughed:

"You don't just walk hup to a Negro, especially one what's passin', and say, 'Ain't you master so-and-so's boy?' No, it's a more delicate, difficult hunt." Here he stared into his cup. "When you *really* after a man with a price on his head, you forgit for the hunt that you the hunter. You get hup at the

Lois M. Jones '72

cracka dawn and creep ovah to where that Negro is hidin'. It ain't so much in overpowerin' him physically, when you huntin' a Negro, as it is mentally. Yo mind has to soak hup his mind. His heart." Here he shogged down a mouthful of corn and cringed. "The Negro-hunt depends on how you use destiny. You let destiny outrace and nail down the Negro you after. From the get-go, hours afore Ah spot him, there's this thing Ah do, like throwin' mah voice. Ah calls his name. The name his master used. *Andrew*, Ah says, if his name be Andrew; *Andrew*." I stiffened inwardly, but gave no sign. "Mah feelin's, and my voice, fly out to fasten onto that Negro. He senses me afore he sees me. You *become* a Negro by lettin' yoself see what he sees, feel what he feels, want what he wants. What does he want?" The Soulcatcher winked at Reb, who was brutally silent, chipped from stone. "Respectability. In his bones he wants to be able to walk down the street and be unnoticed—not *ignored*, which means you seen him and looked away, but unnoticed like people who have a right to be somewheres. He wants what them poets hate: mediocrity. A tame, teacup-passin', uneventful life. Not to go against the law but hug it. A comfortable, hardworkin' life among the Many. Don't seem like much to ask, do it?" This he put to Reb; my friend did not answer. But this, too, was an answer. "It wears him down, ya know? Investin' so much to get so little. It starts showin'. You look for the man who's policin' hisself, tryin' his level best to be *average*. That's yo Negro." Here he held his cup in both hands. "You nail his soul so he can't slip away. Even 'fore he knows you been watchin' him, he's already in leg irons. When you really onto him, the only person who knows he's

Ubi Girl from Tai Region, by Lois Mailou Jones, 1972.

a runaway—almost somebody he kin trust—you tap him gently on his shoulder, and he knows; it's the Call he's waited for his whole life. His capture happens like a wish, somethin' he wants, a destiny that come from inside him, not outside. And me, Ah'm just Gawd's instrument for this, Master Harris, his humble tool, and Ah never finish the kill 'til the prey desires hit."

I said nothing. He did not find me ripe for plucking; he would wait—if his tale could be trusted—until I turned my neck toward the knife. It was a bizarre story, the strangest yet in this odyssey, but it explained (for me) Bannon's Negroid speech, his black idiosyncrasies, tics absorbed from the countless bondsmen he'd assassinated.

"The hunt," said Bannon, suddenly, "is also sweetah when you give the prey a li'l room to run. If Ah ever meet a Negro Ah can't catch, Ah'll quit!"

"Horace," I said, nodding to Reb, "my man and I will travel tonight after all. We've put you out, and I think we can make Spartanburg by daybreak."

"Then Ah'll break camp and take you." Bannon stood quickly, dusting off the seat of his trousers. "Wouldn't do to travel on foot, sick as you look. Besides, Ah know a doctor there—no butchering veterinarian—who kin see to yo bruises." He whipped out a pearl-handled, single-shot derringer, the sort of pistol a brothel keeper might conceal in his boot, from his pocket, played with it, pointed it at me, but remained as polite and unthreatening as a colored preacher talking to the Devil. "Do you know how Ah bagged my fust Negro passin' fo' white?"

I gazed diagonally across the fire at him. The Soulcatcher made another stage wait. Then:

"He lit out from a farm in Wareshoals and reestablished hisself in Due West. Got pretty good at passin', too. They give him this job at a factory. You know what happened?" Bannon grinned; he had four—maybe five—gumline cavities. "His foreman asked him to work on a holiday. This Negro thought on it a spell. He said, 'If'n the Lord's willin', and if Ah sees next sweet potato pickin' time.' Might's well as hung a sign round his neck, sayin' somethin' as bootblack as that." The Soulcatcher, slapping his knee, howled.

My polite laughter rang false, even to me—a timed laugh I'd perfected at Leviathan, which I let linger for a few breaths.

The Soulcatcher only smiled. They lifted me, cloak and all, into the back of the buckboard, and, as Bannon threw dirt on his campfire, Reb pulled the thick tarpaulin over me slowly in order to whisper, "Andrew"—the Coffinmaker only called me Andrew when scared or feeling sappy— "you ain't goin' off with this lunatic, are you?"

"Do we have a choice?"

MARILYN WANIEK

Poet Marilyn Waniek, whose father was a Tuskegee Airman and one of the nation's first black pilots, often writes about the military experiences of African Americans before the armed forces were desegregated. In this poem, she explores some of the disadvantages *of coming out from behind the veil of race. The speaker, Waniek's "one blood-uncle," recalls how integrating the army during the final days of World War II meant going from "three men in a tent" to "one of us . . . four of them."*

THREE MEN IN A TENT

For Rufus C. Mitchell

My one blood-uncle laughs
and shakes his handsome head.
Yeah, that was Ol' Corbon.
He was your daddy's classmate,
you know: They went to school together
at Wilberforce.

    Seemed like Ol' Corbon
    was in trouble all the time.
    We slept two guys to a tent,
    you know, and seemed like nobody
    wanted to bunk with Ol' Corbon.
    He was such a hard-luck case;
    the guys thought he was jinxed.

    Finally, he came to me and Dillard
    —Dillard was my tent-mate—
    and asked if he could bunk with us,
    because he knew your dad.
    He said he'd sleep
    at the foot of our tent.
    Dillard said, *Shit, man,*
    but I talked him over.

    We were on Cape Bon, Tunisia,
    you know, and we had to take turns
    doing guard-duty.
    The Germans parachuted soldiers in
    almost every night,

and they knifed men
sleeping in their tents.

One night it was Ol' Corbon's turn,
and he fell asleep on duty.
You know,
you can be shot
for that during combat.
But Ol' Corbon bailed himself out;
he bought life
with his black mother-wit.

The water there
was corroding the cooling systems.
If they rusted too much,
the planes couldn't fly.
Most of the pilots
—Negro and white—
were just sitting around.
The ground-crews were going crazy,
but what could we do?
You had to use water,
and the corrosive water
was the only water we had.

Then Ol' Corbon remembered
that they'd had to build a distillery
to make distilled water
for the chemistry lab at Wilberforce.
Hey, man, he told me,
I think we can do that.
So we rag-patched one together

and got our boys
back in the air.

The Commanding Officer came over
to find out why the colored boys could fly,
and Ol' Corbon explained our distillery.

Then there were the spark-plug cleaners.
You know, it's easy in the States
to clean spark plugs:
you just use a spark-plug cleaner.
But we didn't have spark-plug cleaners;
they were back in the States.
The planes were grounded again
while we waited.
Thirty to sixty days,
they said it would take.

But Ol' Corbon said
Hey, man,
I bet we can make one.
You want to try?

Well, it turns out
to be pretty simple
to make a spark-plug cleaner.
You just take a big can,
fill it with desert sand,
make a space at the top
for a spark plug,
and blast high-pressure air
through a hole in the side.

You know, the first time
I saw General Eisenhower
was when he flew in
to find out why
the 99th was flying.

The CO introduced Staff Sergeant Corbon.

A little while later
Cape Bon Airfield
was integrated.
We were five men to a tent:
one of us
to four
of them.

I sure missed
my old buddies.
I even missed
Ol' Corbon.

PATRICIA WILLIAMS

The complex interaction of law and race in America is the subject of Patricia Williams's 1991 book The Alchemy of Race and Rights: Diary of a Law Professor. *In the following paragraphs, the rage for "buzzing" customers into fancy New York shops is matched only by the rage of those whom the buzzer system excludes. Professor Williams's experience at one shop during the Christmas season recalls Du Bois's veil—transparent but unyielding—and the dangerous anger it arouses.*

BUZZERS

Buzzers are big in New York City. Favored particularly by smaller stores and boutiques, merchants throughout the city have installed them as screening devices to reduce the incidence of robbery: if the face at the door looks desirable, the buzzer is pressed and the door is unlocked. If the face is that of an undesirable, the door stays locked. Predictably, the issue of undesirability has revealed itself to be a racial determination. While controversial enough at first, even civil-rights organizations backed down eventually in the face of arguments that the buzzer system is a "necessary evil," that it is a "mere inconvenience" in comparison to the risks of being murdered, that suffering discrimination is not as bad as being assaulted, and that in any event it is not all blacks who are barred, just "17-year-old black males wearing running shoes and hooded sweatshirts."

The installation of these buzzers happened swiftly in New York; stores that had always had their doors wide open suddenly became exclusive or received people by appointment only. I discovered them and their meaning one Saturday in 1986. I was shopping in Soho and saw in a store window a sweater that I wanted to buy for my mother. I pressed my round brown face to the window and my finger to the buzzer, seeking admittance. A narrow-eyed, white teenager wearing running shoes and feasting on bubble gum glared out, evaluating me for signs that would pit me against the limits of his social understanding. After about five seconds, he mouthed "We're closed," and blew pink rubber at me. It was two Saturdays before Christmas, at one

Window Shopper, by Aaron Douglas © 1930 *(Collection of Reba and Dave Williams)*

o'clock in the afternoon; there were several white people in the store who appeared to be shopping for things for *their* mothers.

I was enraged. At that moment I literally wanted to break all the windows of the store and *take* lots of sweaters for my mother. In the flicker of his judgmental gray eyes, that saleschild had transformed my brightly sentimental, joy-to-theworld, pre-Christmas spree to a shambles. He snuffed my sense of humanitarian catholicity, and there was nothing I could do to snuff his, without making a spectacle of myself.

SAMUEL DELANY

Science-fiction writer Samuel Delany also takes as his subject the anger of the excluded in his recent novel, Stars in My Pocket like Grains of Sand. *In the following scene, two men confront each other across a circular desk. The man who sits at the center of the desk wears a strange mask that seems almost alive, a character in its own right, like Du Bois's veil. Though race is never mentioned, we recognize its presence in this futuristic encounter.*

THE MAN IN THE WIRE-FILAMENT MASK

"Of course," they told him in all honesty, "you will be a slave."

His big-pored forehead wrinkled, his heavy lips opened (the flesh around his green, green eyes stayed exactly the same), the ideogram of incomprehension among whose radicals you could read ignorance's determinant past, information's present impossibility, speculation's denied future.

"But you will be happy," the man in the wire-filament mask went on from the well in the circle desk. "Certainly you will be happier than you are." The features moved behind pink and green plastic lozenges a-shake on shaking wires. "I mean, look at you, boy. You're ugly as mud and tall enough to scare children in the street. The prenatal brain damage, small as it is, we still can't correct. You've been in trouble of one sort or another for as long as there are records on you: orphanages, foster homes, youth rehabilitation camps, adult detention units—and *you* haven't gotten along in any of them. Sexually . . . ?" Lozenge tinkled against lozenge; the man's head shook. "In this part of the world your preferences in that area can't have done you any good. You're a burden to yourself, to your city, to your geosector." Lozenges lowered, just a bit: the man moved forward in his seat. "But we can change all that."

He pushed back in the sling that was uncomfortable and costly. A blank and intricate absence on his face, he raised one big-knuckled hand to point with a finger thick as a broom handle—for the technology of that world still made lathes, lasers, bombs, and brooms: the nail was gnawed almost off it, as were the nails on his other fingers and thumbs. Crowding his wide palms' edge, whether flailing before him or loose in his lap, those fingers seemed not only too rough and too heavy for any gentle gesture, but also— though, if you counted, there were only ten—too many. The finger (not the fore- but the middle) jabbed brutally, futilely. "You can change me?" The voice in his nineteen-year-old throat was harsh as some fifty-year-old derelict's.

"You can make me like you? Go on! Make me so I can understand things and numbers and reading and stuff!" As brutally, the finger came back against the horse-boned jaw; a mutated herpes virus, along with some sex-linked genetic anomaly, had, until three years ago when the proper phage was developed, rendered the ordinary adolescent acne of the urban males in that world's lower latitudes a red, pitted disaster. "All right, change me! Make me like you!"

Either side of a plastic diamond, the mouth's corners rose. "We could." The plastic swung with breath. "But if we did, then you wouldn't really *be* you anymore, now, would you?" From the black ceiling, through the orrery of masking bits, a hanging lamp dappled the man's naked arms. "We're going to make a change in your mind—a change in your brain—a very small change, a change much smaller than the one you just asked for. We're going to take that little knot of anger you just waved at me on the end of your finger, that anger you just threw back at your own face—we're going to take that knot and we're going to untie it."

CONNIE PORTER

Mikey, the hero of Connie Porter's 1991 novel All-Bright Court, *is an African-American student in a private—and mostly white—prep school. Like James Baldwin's "G.," Mikey often feels alone, but the discomfort he endures is internal, a widening rift between himself and his loving family. The following passage, which contrasts Mikey's new learning with his father's wisdom, gives a humorous meaning to "double-consciousness."*

MIKEY'S NEW SCHOOL

Early on, what Mikey was learning seemed to bring about a beauty in him, a softness. He was put in a speech class where he was taught formal conversation. He listened to tapes entitled "Verb Tense," "Possession," "Agreement." He learned to release his vowels, to round them and pop them out of his mouth. It seemed unnatural to him at first, and he felt almost a little guilty, a little embarrassed when he practiced retaining his *-ing's*.

"Think of it as a game, like juggling eggs," Mikey's speech teacher had said. "If you keep them all in the air, you'll dazzle the audience, but if you drop one, you'll make a mess."

Mikey kept his teacher's analogy in mind, and practiced not dropping his *-ing's*.

No one at school dropped them. None of the boys were constantly making messes of themselves. Mikey listened to them speak in class. He heard the joking in the cafeteria and the locker room. In these two places it seemed a boy could make a mess, a boy might be expected to make a mess. But the other boys never dropped their eggs. The two older black boys he had seen never dropped their eggs either, even when Mikey saw them speaking to each other.

Mikey wondered at them, he wondered about them. He wondered if they had ever spoken like him, and where it was they came from, and how it was they looked so comfortable. They spoke with no effort, it seemed, when he had to think about everything he said. Mikey wanted to sound like them, to look like them, to walk up and down the halls with the white boys and talk about skiing and sleep-overs. But both of these boys were in the seventh grade, while he was in the fourth, and they appeared each day with short, neatly brushed hair that had very little grease. And they showed a remarkable talent for juggling.

It was Mikey who dropped his eggs. It was Mikey who broke enough in one sentence to make himself an omelet.

"Practice" is what his speech teacher told him. "Practice at home when you speak with your family members."

And that was what Mikey did. At the dinner table he would not say, "We be havin' fun in gym class," but "I had fun in gym class today."

Or, "When I was riding home today with Mrs. Cox, I saw a tanker out on the lake."

Dorene would tease him. "Listen to him talk with all that proper talk. All the time now you be trying to talk like a white boy."

But his parents would come to his defense. "Just cut that out," one of them would say. "Ain't nothing wrong with the way he talk. That's the right way to talk. The rest of ya'll should try to talk that way too."

Mikey's parents were proud of the way he spoke. He was smart and getting smarter, sounding smarter. They never corrected him when he made a mistake. They didn't know how. His parents could both see the learning was changing him, but so was the unlearning.

They did not know that during his second semester at Essex, Mikey had told a boy what his father said about monkeys.

Mikey was six when his father told him. They had been in the monkey house at the Buffalo Zoo. His mother had refused to go inside, and waited out front with Dorene and Mary.

Inside, his father said, "I'm telling you, don't pay no attention to they screaming. They smart, smart enough to talk. But they won't, 'cause if they do, they know white people going to make them work."

"Is that true, Daddy?" Mikey asked.

"Yeah, it's true. My daddy told me so."

Mikey had repeated the story to a boy named Scott in the school cafeteria. They had been studying evolution. He was careful to watch his diction, and censor the part about white people. He said only, "People will put them to work."

But Scott laughed at him. He laughed so hard, he spat out a mouthful of butterscotch pudding.

"You're not serious, are you?" he asked. "Your dad isn't really stupid enough to believe that?"

"No," Mikey said. "It's just a story he told me. Please don't tell anybody."

"Why not? I think it's funny," Scott said.

Despite Mikey's request, Scott repeated the story to the whole science class. Even the teacher laughed. "That's an amusing story, Michael. We all know primates have intelligence, but they have not evolved quite that far yet," the teacher said.

Mikey was embarrassed, but he kept it covered. He kept it covered at home, too, when his father asked what he had studied at school that day. He told him they had studied evolution.

"Man didn't come from monkeys. Don't let them white people tell you that. If they want to believe they came from

monkeys, fine. But don't you believe you came from them,"
his father said.

"But we were studying Darwin, and he says—"

"Don't tell me what he say. I know what he say. I'm not
stupid, you know. Sometime I think you don't believe nobody got sense but you. If you so smart, answer me this. If
man came from them, why there still monkeys? And what
monkeys turning into?"

"I don't know," Mikey said.

"You think them monkeys in the zoo turning into men?"

"I don't know," Mikey said. "No. No, they are not becom-
ing men."

His father said, "Damn right. They smarter than men.
Laying up in zoos all over the world, got white men feeding
them. Just because they in them cages don't mean they don't
got no sense," his father said, and he laughed.

And Mikey wanted to tell him. He wanted to say to his
father, "You're not really stupid enough to believe that!" He
wanted to take his father's laughter away. He was smarter
than his father, and he was angered by his stupid, trick
questions.

Mikey did not understand that his father was not laughing
at him. He was laughing at the beauty, the simplicity of his
fresh-faced cocoa boy.

JAY WRIGHT

When a baffled reader once told Jay Wright that he was
weaving a lot of things together in his work, Wright an-
swered that he was simply uncovering the weave already
there. In language of great complexity and beauty, contem-

porary poet Wright offers his careful reader a glimpse of the new world's cultural tapestry. In this recent poem about desire and death, Du Bois's veil is "interwoven" with other legendary coverings: the veil with which St. Veronica wiped Christ's brow as he climbed Calvary, and which afterward bore the miraculous likeness of his face; the bullfighter's red cape, flourished in the climactic pass known as the "veronica"; the sunset itself, whose "veronica'd blood promises consonance" to the double-consciousness of human desire.

VEIL, I

There is something about the blood in a sunset
that answers no questions;
the tarnished veil of a halo refers us
to a dream we never had;
and whatever wakes in us
when the unseen loon calls
offers no consolation.
Can I speak of the heart here,
when nothing speaks to it?
Can the night's brush uncover crystals of longing
that master moon hides and rocks in the beech?
Given such suspicion,
it is too early to submit to the darkness.
You must commit yourself to the light's weave,
the distant clarity of a promise you may have misunderstood.
Go on;
the sunset's veronica'd blood
promises consonance.
You will learn the veil's appeal to the light in you.

PART TWO

TEXTS OF WATER, SONGS OF EXILE

/\/\

Shuttles in the rocking loom of history,
The dark ships move, the dark ships move . . .
           —*Robert Hayden, "Middle Passage"*

Deep river, my home is over Jordan,
Deep river, Lord, I want to cross over into campground.
           —*Spiritual*

Over my head, I hear music in the air,
There must be a God, somewhere.
           —*Spiritual*

In the language of circle and veil, African-American writers have explored the possibility—and the difficulty—of community in America. In what the poet Michael Harper has called "the text of water," they have sounded the theme of exile.

Like the circle, water is a universal symbol that also carries very particular meanings in African-American culture. In the West African worldview, a watery abyss separates the worlds of the living and the ancestors. To enter the unseen world, the dead must first cross over water. This belief was powerfully enlarged for West Africans kidnapped into slavery, for to reach the Americas they also had to cross over water, the Atlantic Ocean of Middle Passage—the so-called second, or "middle," leg of the infamous Triangle Trade.

As poet Robert Hayden wrote, it was a "voyage through death to life upon these shores." Slave traders crammed as many people as they could between the decks of their ships, knowing that a certain number would die during the passage. And die they did: of suffocation, injury, illness, and despair. Brought upon deck for fresh air, some jumped overboard to their deaths. Those who survived, to be sold as slaves in ports throughout the Americas, knew that they would never see their homes again. Like the dead, they had entered an unseen world across the water.

In the folktale of the Flying Africans, a man brought to America in Middle Passage whispers magic words in the ears of his fellow slaves, who rise up and fly back across the water to Africa. The story expresses the deep wish of captive Africans to return to their homes. In many places, legends persist of Africans who long ago died—or took their lives—while facing east, so that their souls would travel back across the water. In the earliest days of slavery in Truro, Massachusetts, an African man called Pompey climbed a hill with his eating bowl and hanged himself, facing east across the Atlantic. The place where he took his life, prepared to join his ancestors, is still called Pomp's Hill.

As the years wore on, Africans became African Americans. They buried their dead on this side of the water, and gave birth to their children in an exile that was—and was not—home. Although coming from many different West African

cultures, they discovered among themselves common practices and beliefs. Adapted to American conditions, these
gave common meaning to their experiences and thus served
to bring a new community into being.

For African Americans, as for their African forebearers,
water remained a symbol of death and exile even when it
served to baptise them into Christianity. The waters that
flowed between the worlds of the living and the ancestors,
the waters that parted those enslaved on American shores
from home and kin in West Africa—these mingled with the
cleansing waters of baptism in which the Christian convert
was symbolically drowned and saved. In time, the Christian
idea of salvation also mingled with the idea of freedom,
which often lay just across water in the free soil beyond the
Ohio River or the Chesapeake Bay. Heaven—the world of
the ancestors, the land over water—drew as near as the
nearest free state, to which one's kinfolk may have already
escaped.

The first texts of water appeared in spirituals, songs in
which slaves celebrated their faith in an afterlife along with
their hope of freedom in this one. To die and go to heaven,
to rejoin one's kin, to be saved, to return home, to escape to
freedom—these were all one in the language of the spirituals, crossings from one shore to another.

Many biblical stories found their way into the spirituals,
but none is more richly represented than that of Moses and
the Israelites. Enslaved men and women identified whole-
heartedly with the biblical people whom God delivered
from bondage in Egypt and set wandering in the desert for
forty years before finally leading them across the Jordan

River into the Promised Land. Remembering this history, and ever mindful of the American waters that lay between them and freedom, slaves sang of "Jordan River, chilly and cold" and the family gone ahead to the other side, of "one more river to cross," and of a "deep river" and the wish to "cross over into campground." For those who sang as well as those who listened, the crossing meant simultaneously death, salvation, and escape to freedom.

From the Bible, enslaved men and women took not only the hope of deliverance and justice, but also the promise of a guiding voice in their exile. In the spirituals they created just such a voice. During the long years of slavery, hope must have failed many times, but the songs themselves were there to "cheer the weary traveller," a "music in the air" that was itself a sign of God's presence.

In the spirituals, water and song are knotted together in a complex tangle of meanings having to do with loss and exile, consolation and hope. This tangle, present at the very outset of African-American culture, remains today in the work of many writers, as you will discover in reading the following selections. Some of these explore the water of Middle Passage and exile, others the water separating slavery from freedom. Still others celebrate the music that has guided African Americans, and other Americans, through the wilderness on this side of the water.

THE TEXT OF WATER, I: MIDDLE PASSAGE

◎

ROBERT HAYDEN

Of the many who died in Middle Passage, only a few entered the historical record, and only then as lost property. *This is what the poet Robert Hayden discovered in the New York Public Library during the early 1940s when he did the research for his epic poem,* Middle Passage. *Slavetraders insured their human goods, and when all or part of a cargo was lost they filed insurance claims and testimony was taken. The following stanzas from* Middle Passage *are based on the testimony of one sailor aboard the doomed slave ship* The Bella J. *In reconstructing his words, Hayden emphasizes the horror of the sailor's remembrance as well as the irony of treating human beings as insurable property.*

THE SAILOR'S TESTIMONY

"Deponent further sayeth *The Bella J*
left the Guinea Coast
with cargo of five hundred blacks and odd
for the barracoons of Florida:

"That there was hardly room 'tween-decks for half
the sweltering cattle stowed spoon-fashion there;
that some went mad of thirst and tore their flesh
and sucked the blood:

"That Crew and Captain lusted with the comeliest
of the savage girls kept naked in the cabins;
that there was one they called The Guinea Rose
and they cast lots and fought to lie with her:

"That when the Bo's'n piped all hands, the flames
spreading from starboard already were beyond
control, the negroes howling and their chains
entangled with the flames:

"That the burning blacks could not be reached,
that the Crew abandoned ship,
leaving their shrieking negresses behind,
that the Captain perished drunken with the wenches:

"Further Deponent sayeth not."

JOHN WIDEMAN

*John Wideman's recent short story "Fever" is based on the
epidemics of yellow fever and dengue that raged through
New Orleans in the final years of the eighteenth century.
People claimed that these diseases were brought to New
Orleans by those fleeing the slave-led revolution in Santo
Domingo (present-day Haiti). The story's speaker, an old
slave who is himself a survivor of Middle Passage, knows
better: It is the moral infection of buying and selling human
beings that is killing the people of New Orleans.*

FEVER

All things arrive in the waters and waters carry all things away. So there is no beginning or end, only the waters' flow, ebb, flood, trickle, tides emptying and returning, salt seas and rivers and rain and mist and blood, the sun drowning in an ocean of night, wet sheen of dawn washing darkness from our eyes. This city is held in the water's palm. A captive as surely as I am captive. Long fingers of river, Schuylkill, Delaware, the rest of the hand invisible; underground streams and channels feed the soggy flesh of marsh, clay pit, sink, gutter, stagnant pool. What's not seen is heard in the suck of footsteps through spring mud of unpaved streets. Noxious vapors that sting your eyes, cause you to gag, spit and wince are evidence of a presence, the dead hand cupping this city, the poisons that circulate through it, the sweat on its rotting flesh.

No one has asked my opinion. No one will. Yet I have seen this fever before, and though I can prescribe no cure, I could tell stories of other visitations, how it came and stayed and left us, the progress of disaster, its several stages, its horrors and mitigations. My words would not save one life, but those mortally affrighted by the fever, by the prospect of universal doom, might find solace in knowing there are limits to the power of this scourge that has befallen us, that some, yea, most will survive, that this condition is temporary, a season, that the fever must disappear with the first deep frosts and its disappearance is as certain as the fact it will come again.

They say the rat's-nest ships from Santo Domingo brought the fever. Frenchmen and their black slaves fleeing black insurrection. Those who've seen Barbados's distemper say our fever is its twin born in the tropical climate of the hellish Indies. I know better. I hear the drum, the forest's heartbeat, pulse of the sea that chains the moon's wandering, the spirit's journey. Its throb is source and promise of all things being connected, a mirror storing everything, forgetting nothing. To explain the fever we need no boatloads of refugees, ragged and wracked with killing fevers, bringing death to our shores. We have bred the affliction within our breasts. Each solitary heart contains all the world's tribes, and its precarious dance echoes the drum's thunder. We are our ancestors and our children, neighbors and strangers to ourselves. Fever descends when the waters that connect us are clogged with filth. When our seas are garbage. The waters cannot come and go when we are shut off one from the other, each in his frock coat, wig, bonnet, apron, shop, shoes, skin, behind locks, doors, sealed faces, our blood grows thick and sluggish. Our bodies void infected fluids. Then we are dry and cracked as a desert country, vital parts wither, all dust and dry bones inside. Fever is a drought consuming us from within. Discolored skin caves in upon itself, we burn, expire.

I regret there is so little comfort in this explanation. It takes into account neither climatists nor contagionists, flies in the face of logic and reason, the good doctors of the College of Physicians who would bleed us, purge us, quar-antine, plunge us in icy baths, starve us, feed us elixirs of bark and wine, sprinkle us with gunpowder, drown us in vinegar according to the dictates of their various healing sciences. Who, then, is this foolish, old man who receives his wisdom from pagan drums in pagan forests? Are these the delusions of one whose brain the fever has already begun to gnaw? Not quite. True, I have survived other visitations of the fever, but while it prowls this city, I'm in jeopardy again as you are, because I claim no immunity, no magic. The messenger who bears the news of my death will reach me precisely at the stroke determined when it was determined I should tumble from the void and taste air the first time. Nothing is an accident. Fever grows in the secret places of our hearts, planted there when one of us decided to sell one of us to another. The drum must pound ten thousand thousand years to drive that evil away.

JAMAICA KINCAID

Jamaica Kincaid's 1990 novel Lucy *tells the story of a young West Indian woman who comes to Chicago to work as a nanny. She arrives in the middle of January and is astonished by what she finds. In this paragraph, Lucy speaks of the rift opening between her new life and her past in language that recalls Middle Passage. For Kincaid, as for other writers, the historical event is never far from recollection and can be summoned forth by something as mundane as winter weather.*

LEAVING HOME

That morning, the morning of my first day, the morning that followed my first night, was a sunny morning. It was not the sort of bright sun-yellow making everything curl at the edges, almost in fright, that I was used to, but a pale-yellow sun, as if the sun had grown weak from trying too hard to shine; but still it was sunny, and that was nice and made me miss my home less. And so, seeing the sun, I got up and put on a dress, a gay dress made out of madras cloth—the same sort of dress that I would wear if I were at home and setting out for a day in the country. It was all wrong. The sun was shining but the air was cold. It was the middle of January, after all. But I did not know that the sun could shine and the air remain cold; no one had ever told me. What a feeling that was! How can I explain? Something I had always known—the way I knew my skin was the color brown of a nut rubbed repeatedly with a soft cloth, or the way I knew my own name—something I took completely for granted, "the sun is shining, the air is warm," was not so. I was no longer in a tropical zone, and this realization now entered my life like a flow of water dividing formerly dry and solid ground, creating two banks, one of which was my past—so familiar and predictable that even my unhappiness then made me happy now just to think of it—the other my future, a gray blank, an overcast seascape on which rain was falling and no boats were in sight. I was no longer in a tropical zone and I felt cold inside and out, the first time such a sensation had come over me.

CALVIN FORBES

For Calvin Forbes, as for Jamaica Kincaid, cold weather and Middle Passage are deeply connected. In his poem "Blue Monday," a weekend blues artist returns to the bondage of work in Eskimo city, feeling as if "he's been below deck all his life." The moaning stranger he is chained to is his workaday self. Here, as in so much African-American writing, water and music are knotted together in a single language.

BLUE MONDAY

Cotton eyes soaking up blood

All alone in Eskimo city
Cold and unsure, the music man

No earth angel, no sissy, brings
The night to its knees. Some-
Times he feels he's been below deck

All his life chained to a stranger
Moaning blue monday where's a calendar

Without weekends. Blue monday he moans
Where's a place where the darkness
Is not a dungeon. Slipping sliding his way

To be alive, he mumbles to his boss.
His soul trails behind him like a sled.

Too weak to work he's tired of playing.

He's gonna rock on the river of time
And stare at God until he goes blind.

MICHAEL HARPER
In this elegy from his 1985 book Healing Song for the Inner
Ear, *poet Michael Harper remembers his younger brother*

Jonathan, killed in a motorcycle accident. "The Drowning of the Facts of a Life" opens on the evening of the day Jonathan's ashes have been scattered in the "waters off Long Beach."

As the family talks of its loss, the poet imagines ashes and flowers still floating together, but has little hope that this "text of water" will be deciphered in a lost nation that cannot even pronounce the names of its killing weapons. In place of America's "foolish talk," the poet offers his own memories—of Jonathan as a child growing up in Brooklyn, and of his final days in a coma.

The poem ends in the hospital room as the poet chants his brother's name, hoping to guide him back to the world of the living. But Jonathan, "apple and brother in the next world," will not be recalled.

THE DROWNING OF
THE FACTS OF A LIFE

Who knows why we talk of death
this evening, warm beyond the measure
of breath; it will be cool tomorrow
for in the waters off Long Beach
my brother's ashes still collect
the flowers of my mother and father,
my sister dropped in the vase
of a face they made of old places,
the text of water.

Tonight we talk of losses in the word
and go on drowning in acts of faith

The Sea Nymph, by Romare Bearden.

knowing so little of humility,
less of the body,
which will die in the mouth of reality.

This foolish talk in a country
that cannot pronounce napalm
or find a path to a pool of irises
or the head of a rose.

My brother was such a flower;
he would spring into my path
on a subway train, above the ground
now, on the way home from school,
letting the swift doors pinch
his fingers of books and records,
house supplies from the corner market,
as he leaped back to the station
platform, crying his pleasure
to his brother,
who was on the train . . .
getting off at next exit
to look for him.

This is how we make our way home:
Each day when the Amtrak express
on the northeast corridor
takes my heritage from Boston
to the everglades of Maryland,
I think of the boy who sat
on the platform in the Canarsie,
on the uneven projects of New Lots
Avenue, BMT:

he was so small he could slip
through the swinging chains
of the express train
on the Williamsburg Bridge,
and not get touched by the third rail,
the chain link fencing of the accordion
swiveling to the swing and curses
of the motorman.

A fortnight my brother lay in coma,
his broken pate and helmet
in a shopping bag of effects,
his torn-off clothes and spattering
coins, the keys to the golden Yamaha—
with remnants of pavement in his scalp,
the trace of jacket laid under his head,
the black Continental idling
at anchor with the infinite,
the same black ice of the subway.

I came to chant over his fungus-
eaten flesh, allergic to his own
sweat, sweeter than the women
and children collecting
in caravan behind him; the Oriental
nurses, so trained in the cadence
of thermometer and brain scan,
came in their green bracelets
and uniforms to relieve him—
a catheter of extract
makes the pomade of his hair

The Cradle, by John Biggers.

disappear, for his lips twitch
in remembrance at impact,
rage at the power of love,
the welcome table and tabernacle
for his broken shoes and helmet.

Ponder the spent name of Jonathan,
apple and brother in the next
world, where the sacred text
of survival is buried in the bosom
of a child, radiated
in moonlight forever.
I touch the clean nostril
of the body in his mechanical
breathing, no chant sound enough
to lift him from the rest
of contraption
to the syncopated dance of his name.

DEREK WALCOTT

According to Nobel Laureate Derek Walcott, "The fate of poetry is to fall in love with the world, in spite of history." We understand something of what that means in this brief passage from Walcott's 1973 poem "The Shell's Howl," which is about voyages of dislocation, especially those which brought people from all over the world to the West Indian islands. As the seashell preserves and transforms "the howls of all the races that crossed the water," so poetry preserves and transforms history, making a song out of exile.

THE SHELL'S HOWL

That child who sets his half-shell afloat
in the brown creek that is Rampanalgas River—
my son first, then two daughters—
towards the roar of waters,
towards the Atlantic with a dead almond leaf for a sail,
with a twig for a mast,
was, like his father, this child,
a child without history, without knowledge of its pre-world,
only the knowledge of water runnelling rocks,
and the desperate whelk that grips the rock's outcrop
like a man whom the waves can never wash overboard;
that child who puts the shell's howl to his ear,
hears nothing, hears everything
that the historian cannot hear, the howls
of all the races that crossed the water,
the howls of grandfathers drowned
in that intricately swivelled Babel,
hears the fellaheen, the Madrasi, the Mandingo, the Ashanti,
yes, and hears also the echoing green fissures of Canton,
and thousands without longing for this other shore
by the mud tablets of the Indian Provinces,
robed ghostly white and brown, the twigs of uplifted hands,
of manacles, mantras, of a thousand kaddishes,
whorled, drilling into the shell,
see, in the evening light by the saffron, sacred Benares,
how they are lifting like herons,
robed ghostly white and brown,
and the crossing of water has erased their memories.
And the sea, which is always the same,
accepts them.

And the shore, which is always the same,
accepts them.

In the shallop of the shell,
in the round prayer,
in the palate of the conch,
in the dead sail of the almond leaf
are all of the voyages.

THE TEXT OF WATER, II: DEEP RIVER

MELVIN DIXON

In this brief tribute to his grandmother, Melvin Dixon invokes the many meanings of water in the African-American tradition and contemplates his own death as well. As his grandmother sinks beneath the waters, the poet imagines her rising "alone on the other side" and reaches out to pull her back. "Grandmother: Crossing Jordan" was written in 1990, two years before Dixon's death from a long illness. Its final stanza seems to ask whether he will be "ready," as she was, when the time comes to cross over.

GRANDMOTHER: CROSSING JORDAN

> Rippling hospital sheets
> circle your brown body
> and you sink
> for the third time,
> ready to rise alone
> on the other side.

I reach out for you
and pull and pull
until your skin tears
from the bones of elbow,
arm, wrist, and fingers.

How it hangs empty,
loose. A glove
too large
for my hand.

CHRISTOPHER GILBERT

If the world of the ancestors lies across water, then as one
grows older, the shores of that world grow closer and closer.
This humorous logic underlies Christopher Gilbert's 1984
poem "This Bridge Across," itself a prayer, or bridge across,
to those who have taught him to live "beyond my self."

THIS BRIDGE ACROSS

A moment comes to me
and it's a lot like the dead
who get in the way sometimes
hanging around, with their ranks
growing bigger by the second
and the game of tag they play
claiming whoever happens by.
I try to put them off
but the space between us
is like a country growing closer

which has a language I know
more and more of me is
growing up inside of, and
the clincher is the nothing
for me to do inside here
except to face my dead
as the spirits they are,
find the parts of me in them—
call them back with my words.
Ancestor worship or prayer?
It's a kind of getting by—
an extension of living
beyond my self my people taught me,
and each moment is a boundary
I will throw this bridge across.

RITA DOVE

Rita Dove's 1986 Thomas and Beulah *celebrates the lives of her grandparents, Southerners who came North in the Great Migration of African Americans before and during World War I. Thomas's journey veers into tragedy when his best friend, Lem, drowns beneath the paddlewheel of the boat carrying them upriver out of the South. Lonely, guilt-ridden, terrified of water, Thomas goes on to find safe passage through life in marriage, fatherhood, and church.*

"Thomas at the Wheel" recounts his fatal heart attack while on his way to the drugstore. Here, death is a drowning, as it was for Lem. The steering wheel recalls not only the wheel of life, which has come full circle for Thomas, but also the paddle wheel beneath which Lem drowned. As Thomas's

lungs fill up with water, he thinks of the prescription for heart medicine in the glove compartment— "the writing on the water," a vanishing text, like his life.

THOMAS AT THE WHEEL

This, then, the river he had to swim.
Through the wipers the drugstore
shouted, lit up like a casino,
neon script leering from the shuddering asphalt.

Then the glass doors flew apart
and a man walked out to the curb
to light a cigarette. Thomas thought
the sky was emptying itself as fast
as his chest was filling with water.

Should he honk? What a joke—
he couldn't ungrip the steering wheel.
The man looked him calmly in the eye
and tossed the match away.

And now the street dark, not a soul
nor its brother. He lay down across
the seat, a pod set to sea,
a kiss unpuckering. He watched
the slit eye of the glove compartment,
the prescription inside,

he laughed as he thought *Oh
the writing on the water.* Thomas imagined
his wife as she awoke missing him,
cracking a window. He heard sirens
rise as the keys swung, ticking.

LANGSTON HUGHES

In 1920, when he was eighteen, Langston Hughes crossed the Mississippi for the first time in his life. The result was "The Negro Speaks of Rivers," one of his earliest and best-known poems, an eloquent reminder that the Mississippi with its "muddy bosom," and the African-American experience itself, are but one portion of Negro history. Langston Hughes dedicated "The Negro Speaks of Rivers" to W.E.B. Du Bois.

THE NEGRO SPEAKS OF RIVERS

I've known rivers:
I've known rivers ancient as the world and older than the
        flow of human blood in human veins.

My soul has grown deep like the rivers.

I bathed in the Euphrates when dawns were young.
I built my hut near the Congo and it lulled me to sleep.
I looked upon the Nile and raised the pyramids above it.
I heard the singing of the Mississippi when Abe Lincoln
        went down to New Orleans, and I've seen its
        muddy bosom turn all golden in the sunset.

I've known rivers:
Ancient, dusky rivers.

My soul has grown deep like the rivers.

RICHARD WRIGHT

A menacing Mississippi River figures in Richard Wright's recollection of Uncle Hoskins in his 1945 autobiography,

Black Boy. *The portrait falls into two distinct parts: Wright's*
terrifying encounter with the river is immediately followed
by the story of his uncle's murder.

Our sense of the symbolic connection between water and
death, water and racial violence, draws the two parts into a
powerful whole.

UNCLE HOSKINS

Uncle Hoskins had a horse and buggy and sometimes he
used to take me with him to Helena, where he traded. One
day when I was riding with him he said:

"Richard, would you like to see this horse drink water out
of the middle of the river?"

"Yes," I said, laughing. "But this horse can't do that."

"Yes, he can," Uncle Hoskins said. "Just wait and see."

He lashed the horse and headed the buggy straight for the
Mississippi River.

"Where're you going?" I asked, alarm mounting in me.

"We're going to the middle of the river so the horse can
drink," he said.

He drove over the levee and down the long slope of
cobblestones to the river's edge and the horse plunged
wildly in. I looked at the mile stretch of water that lay ahead
and leaped up in terror.

"Naw!" I screamed.

"This horse has to drink," Uncle Hoskins said grimly.

"The river's deep!" I shouted.

"The horse can't drink here," Uncle Hoskins said, lashing
the back of the struggling animal.

The buggy went farther. The horse slowed a little and

tossed his head above the current. I grabbed the sides of the buggy, ready to jump, even though I could not swim.

"Sit down or you'll fall out!" Uncle Hoskins shouted.

"Let me out!" I screamed.

The water now came up to the hubs of the wheels of the buggy. I tried to leap into the river and he caught hold of my leg. We were now surrounded by water.

"Let me out!" I screamed.

The buggy rolled on and the water rose higher. The horse wagged his head, arched his neck, flung his tail about, walled his eyes, and snorted. I gripped the sides of the buggy with all the strength I had, ready to wrench free and leap if the buggy slipped deeper into the river. Uncle Hoskins and I tussled.

"Whoa!" he yelled at last to the horse.

The horse stopped and neighed. The swirling yellow water was so close that I could have touched the surface of the river. Uncle Hoskins looked at me and laughed.

"Did you really think that I was going to drive this buggy into the middle of the river?" he asked.

I was too scared to answer; my muscles were so taut that they ached.

"It's all right," he said soothingly.

He turned the buggy around and started back toward the levee. I was still clutching the sides of the buggy so tightly that I could not turn them loose.

"We're safe now," he said.

The buggy rolled onto dry land and, as my fear ebbed, I felt that I was dropping from a great height. It seemed that I could smell a sharp, fresh odor. My forehead was damp and my heart thumped heavily.

"I want to get out," I said.

"What's the matter?" he asked.

"I want to get out!"

"We're back on land now, boy."

"Naw! Stop! I want to get out!"

He did not stop the buggy; he did not even turn his head to look at me; he did not understand. I wrenched my leg free with a lunge and leaped headlong out of the buggy, landing in the dust of the road, unhurt. He stopped the buggy.

"Are you really that scared?" he asked softly.

I did not answer; I could not speak. My fear was gone now and he loomed before me like a stranger, like a man I had never seen before, a man with whom I could never share a moment of intimate living.

"Come on, Richard, and get back into the buggy," he said. "I'll take you home now."

I shook my head and began to cry.

"Listen, son, don't you trust me?" he asked. "I was born on that old river. I know that river. There's stone and brick way down under that water. You could wade out for half a mile and it would not come over your head."

His words meant nothing and I would not re-enter the buggy.

"I'd better take you home," he said soberly.

I started down the dusty road. He got out of the buggy and walked beside me. He did not do his shopping that day and when he tried to explain to me what he had been trying to do in frightening me I would not listen or speak to him. I never trusted him after that. Whenever I saw his face the memory of my terror upon the river would come back, vivid and strong, and it stood as a barrier between us.

Each day Uncle Hoskins went to his saloon in the evenings and did not return home until the early hours of the morning. Like my father, he slept in the daytime, but noise never seemed to bother Uncle Hoskins. My brother and I shouted and banged as much as we liked. Often I would creep into his room while he slept and stare at the big shining revolver that lay near his head, within quick reach of his hand. I asked Aunt Maggie why he kept the gun so close to him and she told me that men had threatened to kill him, white men . . .

One morning I awakened to learn that Uncle Hoskins had not come home from the saloon. Aunt Maggie fretted and worried. She wanted to visit the saloon and find out what had happened, but Uncle Hoskins had forbidden her to

People in a Boat, by Robert Blackburn, 1939. *(Collection of Reba and Dave Williams)*

come to the place. The day wore on and dinnertime came.

"I'm going to find out if anything's happened," Aunt Maggie said.

"Maybe you oughtn't," my mother said. "Maybe it's dangerous."

The food was kept hot on the stove and Aunt Maggie stood on the front porch staring into the deepening dusk. Again she declared that she was going to the saloon, but my mother dissuaded her once more. It grew dark and still he had not come. Aunt Maggie was silent and restless.

"I hope to God the white people didn't bother him," she said.

Later she went into the bedroom and when she came out she whimpered:

"He didn't take his gun. I wonder what could have happened?"

We ate in silence. An hour later there was the sound of heavy footsteps on the front porch and a loud knock came. Aunt Maggie ran to the door and flung it open. A tall black boy stood sweating, panting, and shaking his head. He pulled off his cap.

"Mr. Hoskins . . . he done been shot. Done been shot by a white man," the boy gasped. "Mrs. Hoskins, he dead."

Aunt Maggie screamed and rushed off the porch and down the dusty road into the night.

"Maggie!" my mother screamed.

"Don't you-all go to that saloon," the boy called.

"Maggie!" my mother called, running after Aunt Maggie.

"They'll kill you if you go there!" the boy yelled. "White folks say they'll kill all his kinfolks!"

My mother pulled Aunt Maggie back to the house. Fear

drowned out grief and that night we packed clothes and dishes and loaded them into a farmer's wagon. Before dawn we were rolling away, fleeing for our lives. I learned afterwards that Uncle Hoskins had been killed by whites who had long coveted his flourishing liquor business. He had been threatened with death and warned many times to leave, but he had wanted to hold on a while longer to amass more money. We got rooms in West Helena, and Aunt Maggie and my mother kept huddled in the house all day and night, afraid to be seen on the streets. Finally Aunt Maggie defied her fear and made frequent trips back to Elaine, but she went in secret and at night and would tell no one save my mother when she was going.

There was no funeral. There was no music. There was no period of mourning. There were no flowers. There were only silence, quiet weeping, whispers, and fear. I did not know when or where Uncle Hoskins was buried. Aunt Maggie was not even allowed to see his body nor was she able to claim any of his assets. Uncle Hoskins had simply been plucked from our midst and we, figuratively, had fallen on our faces to avoid looking into that white-hot face of terror that we knew loomed somewhere above us. This was as close as white terror had ever come to me and my mind reeled. Why had we not fought back, I asked my mother, and the fear that was in her made her slap me into silence.

SONGS OF EXILE

W . E . B . D U B O I S

The child of an African-American family generations re-moved from slavery, W.E.B. Du Bois remembered first hear-ing spirituals when he was growing up in Massachusetts: "They came out of the South unknown to me, one by one, and yet at once I knew them as of me and of mine." In 1903, when The Souls of Black Folk *was published, many still claimed that slavery was benign and the slave "careless and happy." For Du Bois, the spirituals spoke otherwise. His is one of the great tributes to the music first brought to Ameri-can shores in the slave ships.*

THE SORROW SONGS

. . . not all the past South, though it rose from the dead, can gainsay the heart-touching witness of these songs. They are the music of an unhappy people, of the children of disap-pointment; they tell of death and suffering and unvoiced longing toward a truer world, of misty wanderings and hid-den ways.

The songs are indeed the siftings of centuries; the music is far more ancient than the words, and in it we can trace here

127

and there signs of development. My grandfather's grand-mother was seized by an evil Dutch trader two centuries ago; and coming to the valleys of the Hudson and Housatonic, black, little, and lithe, she shivered and shrank in the harsh north winds, looked longingly at the hills, and often crooned a heathen melody to the child between her knees . . . The child sang it to his children and they to their children's children, and so two hundred years it has trav-elled down to us and we sing it to our children, knowing as little as our fathers what its words may mean, but knowing well the meaning of its music.

This was primitive African music . . . , the voice of exile.

STERLING BROWN

The singer and water are often connected in the writings of African Americans, and nowhere more beautifully than in Sterling Brown's "Ma Rainey," first published in 1932 in Southern Road.

Ma Rainey, who lived from 1886 to 1939, was one of the first great blues singers. In "Backwater Blues," she sang about the Mississippi floods of the late 1920s that had washed out so many people. In Brown's poem, the river's destructive power is matched by the power of Ma Rainey's singing over her listeners' emotions.

MA RAINEY

I
When Ma Rainey
Comes to town,

Folks from anyplace
Miles aroun',
From Cape Girardeau,
Poplar Bluff,
Flocks in to hear
Ma do her stuff;
Comes flivverin' in,
Or ridin' mules,
Or packed in trains,
Picknickin' fools . . . .
That's what it's like,
Fo' miles on down,
To New Orleans delta
An' Mobile town,
When Ma hits
Anywheres aroun'.

II
Dey comes to hear Ma Rainey from de little river settlements,
From blackbottom cornrows and from lumber camps;
Dey stumble in de hall, jes a-laughin' an' a-cacklin',
Cheerin' lak roarin' water, lak wind in river swamps.

An' some jokers keeps deir laughs a-goin' in de crowded aisles,
An' some folks sits dere waitin' wid deir aches an' miseries,
Till Ma comes out before dem, a-smilin' gold-toofed smiles
An' Long Boy ripples minors on de black an' yellow keys.

III
O Ma Rainey,
Sing yo' song;

Now you's back
Whah you belong,
Git way inside us,
Keep us strong . . . .
O Ma Rainey,
Li'l an' low;
Sing us 'bout de hard luck
Roun' our do';
Sing us 'bout de lonesome road
We mus' go. . . .

IV
I talked to a fellow, an' the fellow say,
"She jes' catch hold of us, somekindaway.
She sang Backwater Blues one day:

> *'It rained fo' days an' de skies was dark as night,*
> *Trouble taken place in de lowlands at night.*

> *'Thundered an' lightened an' the storm begin to roll*
> *Thousan's of people ain't got no place to go.*

> *'Den I went an' stood upon some high ol' lonesome hill.*
> *An' looked down on the place where I used to live.'*

An' den de folks, dey natchally bowed dey heads an' cried,
Bowed dey heavy heads, shet dey moufs up tight an' cried,
An' Ma lef' de stage, an' followed some de folks outside."

Dere wasn't much more de fellow say:
She jes' gits hold of us dataway.

The Banjo Lesson, by Henry O. Tanner, 1893.

G W E N D O L Y N   B R O O K S

In her poem honoring singer, actor, and political activist
Paul Robeson (1898–1976), Brooks exposes the American
tendency to reduce a complex life to a single element. An
outspoken critic of American society and its racism, Robe-
son was hounded by the government as a Communist sym-
pathizer. Yet he is most often associated in the public mind
with a single song, "Old Man River." Brooks's poem ques-
tions the popular taste for this "tearful tale . . . of an old
despond," and reminds us that Robeson's "major Voice"
had many things to tell us of our present condition.

PAUL ROBESON

That time
we all heard it,
cool and clear,
cutting across the hot grit of the day.
The major Voice.
The adult Voice
forgoing Rolling River,
forgoing tearful tale of bale and barge
and other symptoms of an old despond.
Warning, in music-words
devout and large,
that we are each other's
harvest:
we are each other's
business:
we are each other's
magnitude and bond.

AUDRE LORDE

Like Gwendolyn Brooks, poet Audre Lorde is impatient with the public's limited view of the African-American singer. As people reduced the fiery Robeson to a single popular song, so they made contralto Mahalia Jackson (1911–1972) "safe" and "acceptable" by ignoring the source and meaning of her music. In Lorde's poem, the mourners who gather to bemoan the passing of her great voice don't even sing "her favorite song." They speak of her early "hard life" as if it were a thing of the past. Meanwhile, in the city outside, fire silences forever the voices of six black children.

THE DAY THEY
EULOGIZED MAHALIA

The day they eulogized Mahalia
the echoes of her big voice stilled
and the mourners found her
singing out from their sisters' mouths
from their mothers' toughness
from the funky dust in the corners
of Sunday church pews
sweet and dry and simple
and that hated Sunday morning fussed-over feeling
the songs
singing out from their mothers' toughness
would never threaten the lord's retribution
any more.

Now she was safe
acceptable   that big Mahalia

Chicago turned all out
to show her that they cared
but her eyes were closed
And although Mahalia loved our music
nobody sang her favorite song
and while we talked about
what a hard life she had known
and wasn't it too bad Sister Mahalia
didn't have it easier   earlier

SIX BLACK CHILDREN
BURNED TO DEATH IN A DAY CARE CENTER
on the South Side
kept in a condemned house
for lack of funds
firemen found their bodies
like huddled lumps of charcoal
with silent mouths and eyes wide open.

Small and without song
six Black children found a voice in flame
the day the city eulogized Mahalia.

RALPH ELLISON

A mysterious encounter takes place in the following scene from Ralph Ellison's 1952 novel Invisible Man. *Expelled from his college, banished to New York City, Ellison's hero meets Peter Wheatstraw, a blues singer whose strange song suggests the biblical scene of exile as well as Invisible Man's lost southern home. The obliterating water of Middle Passage is recalled in the "rolls of blue paper" Peter Wheatstraw carts away. Rejected plans, lost paradigms, these discarded blueprints are all "written on water." But Peter Wheatstraw's blues survives, a guiding—and riddling—song floating above the wreck of the Invisible Man's plans and schemes.*

PETER WHEATSTRAW, THE BLUEPRINT MAN

Close to the curb ahead I saw a man pushing a cart piled high with rolls of blue paper and heard him singing in a clear ringing voice. It was a blues, and I walked along behind him remembering the times that I had heard such singing at home. It seemed that here some memories slipped around my life at the campus and went far back to things I had long ago shut out of my mind. There was no escaping such reminders.

> "She's got feet like a monkey
> Legs like a frog—Lawd, Lawd!
> But when she starts to loving me
> I holler Whooo, God-dog!
> Cause I loves my baabay,
> Better than I do myself . . ."

And as I drew alongside I was startled to hear him call to me:

"Looka-year, buddy . . ."

"Yes," I said, pausing to look into his reddish eyes.

"Tell me just one thing this very fine morning—Hey! Wait a minute, daddy-o, I'm going your way!"

"What is it?" I said.

"What I want to know is," he said, "is you got the *dog?*"

"Dog? What dog?"

"Sho," he said, stopping his cart and resting it on its support. "That's it. *Who*—" he halted to crouch with one foot on the curb like a country preacher about to pound his Bible—"*got . . . the . . . dog,*" his head snapping with each word like an angry rooster's.

I laughed nervously and stepped back. He watched me out of shrewd eyes. "Oh goddog, daddy-o," he said with a sudden bluster, "who got the damn dog? Now I know you from down home, how come you trying to act like you never heard that before! Hell, ain't nobody out here this morning but us colored— Why you trying to deny me?"

Suddenly I was embarrassed and angry. "Deny you? What do you mean?"

"Just answer the question. Is you got him, or ain't you?"

"A *dog?*"

"Yeah, *the* dog."

I was exasperated. "No, not this morning," I said and saw a grin spread over his face.

"Wait a minute, daddy. Now don't go get mad. Damn, man! I thought sho *you* had him," he said, pretending to disbelieve me. I started away and he pushed the cart beside me. And suddenly I felt uncomfortable. Somehow he was like one of the vets from the Golden Day . . .

"Well, maybe it's the other way round," he said. "Maybe he got holt to you."

"Maybe," I said.

"If he is, you lucky it's just a dog—'cause, man, I tell you I believe it's a bear that's got holt to me . . ."

"A bear?"

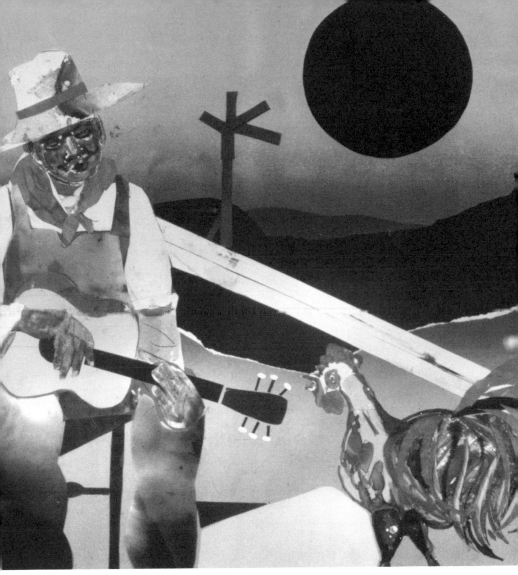

Blues at the Crossroads, by Romare Bearden.

"Hell, yes! *The* bear. Caint you see these patches where he's been clawing at my behind?"

Pulling the seat of his Charlie Chaplin pants to the side, he broke into deep laughter.

"Man, this Harlem ain't nothing but a bear's den. But I tell you one thing," he said with swiftly sobering face, "it's the best place in the world for you and me, and if times don't get better soon I'm going to grab that bear and turn him every way but loose!"

"Don't let him get you down," I said.

"No, daddy-o, I'm going to start with one my own size!"

I tried to think of some saying about bears to reply, but remembered only Jack the Rabbit, Jack the Bear . . . who were both long forgotten and now brought a wave of homesickness. I wanted to leave him, and yet I found a certain comfort in walking along beside him, as though we'd walked this way before through other mornings, in other places . . .

"What is all that you have there?" I said, pointing to the rolls of blue paper stacked in the cart.

"Blueprints, man. Here I got 'bout a hundred pounds of blueprints and I couldn't build nothing!"

"What are they blueprints for?" I said.

"Damn if I know—everything. Cities, towns, country clubs. Some just buildings and houses. I got damn near enough to build me a house if I could live in a paper house like they do in Japan. I guess somebody done changed their plans," he added with a laugh. "I asked the man why they getting rid of all this stuff and he said they get in the way so every once in a while they have to throw 'em out to make place for the new plans. Plenty of these ain't never been used, you know."

"You have quite a lot," I said.

"Yeah, this ain't all neither. I got a coupla loads. There's a day's work right here in this stuff. Folks is always making plans and changing 'em."

"Yes, that's right," I said, thinking of my letters, "but that's a mistake. You have to stick to the plan."

He looked at me, suddenly grave. "You kinda young, daddy-o," he said.

I did not answer. We came to a corner at the top of a hill.

"Well, daddy-o, it's been good talking with a youngster from the old country but I got to leave you now. This here's one of them good ole downhill streets. I can coast a while and won't be worn out at the end of the day. Damn if I'm-a let 'em run *me* into my grave. I be seeing you again sometime— And you know something?"

"What's that?"

"I thought you was trying to deny me at first, but now I be pretty glad to see you . . ."

"I hope so," I said. "And you take it easy."

"Oh, I'll do that. All it takes to get along in this here man's town is a little shit, grit and mother-wit. And man, I was bawn with all three. In fact, I'maseventhsonofaseventhson-bawnwithacauloverbotheyesandraisedonblackcatbones-highjohntheconquerorandgreasygreens—" he spieled with twinkling eyes, his lips working rapidly. "You dig me, daddy?"

"You're going too fast," I said, beginning to laugh.

"Okay, I'm slowing down. I'll verse you but I won't curse you—My name is Peter Wheatstraw, I'm the Devil's only son-in-law, so roll 'em! You a southern boy, ain't you?" he said, his head to one side like a bear's.

"Yes," I said.

"Well, git with it! My name's Blue and I'm coming at you with a pitchfork. Fe Fi Fo Fum. Who wants to shoot the Devil one, Lord God Stingeroy!"

He had me grinning despite myself. I liked his words though I didn't know the answer. I'd known the stuff from childhood, but had forgotten it; had learned it back of school . . .

"You digging me, daddy?" he laughed. "Haw, but look me up sometimes, I'm a piano player and a rounder, a whiskey drinker and a pavement pounder. I'll teach you some good bad habits. You'll need 'em. Good luck," he said.

"So long," I said and watched him going. I watched him push around the corner to the top of the hill, leaning sharp against the cart handle, and heard his voice arise, muffled now, as he started down.

> She's got feet like a monkeeee
> Legs
> Legs, Legs like a maaad
> Bulldog . . .

What does it mean, I thought. I'd heard it all my life but suddenly the strangeness of it came through to me. Was it about a woman or about some strange sphinxlike animal? Certainly his woman, *no* woman, fitted that description. And why describe anyone in such contradictory words? Was it a sphinx? Did old Chaplin-pants, old dusty-butt, love her or hate her; or was he merely singing? What kind of woman could love a dirty fellow like that, anyway? And how could even *he* love her if she were as repulsive as the song described? I moved ahead. Perhaps everyone loved someone; I didn't know. I couldn't give much thought to love; in order to travel far you had to be detached, and I had the long road back to the campus before me. I strode along, hearing the cartman's song become a lonesome, broad-toned whistle now that flowered at the end of each phrase into a tremulous, blue-toned chord. And in its flutter and swoop I heard the sound of a railroad train highballing it, lonely across the lonely night. He was the Devil's son-in-law, all right, and he was a man who could whistle a three-toned chord . . . God damn, I thought, they're a hell of a people! And I didn't know whether it was pride or disgust that suddenly flashed over me.

ROBERT HAYDEN

The ocean of Middle Passage forms the backdrop for another mysterious encounter in Robert Hayden's 1970 poem "Aunt Jemima of the Ocean Waves." As he watches a carnival show pitched at the water's edge, Hayden's unnamed narrator ponders the ugliness of American stereotypes, racial and otherwise. Disgusted, he turns his back on the American continent to face the sea, but one of the performers has understood his deep sense of exile and steps out of her role to make him a consoling gift. As he listens to her life story, Hayden's narrator begins to understand the woman's true power and identity. As African beauty and wisdom survived Middle Passage to take root in the new world, so Aunt Jemima survives the wreck of her own beauty—survives her present grotesque role as "fake mammy"—bringing her transcendent wisdom to one stranded on the American shore.

AUNT JEMIMA OF
THE OCEAN WAVES

I
Enacting someone's notion of themselves
(and me), The One And Only Aunt Jemima
and Kokimo The Dixie Dancing Fool
do a bally for the freak show.

I watch a moment, then move on,
pondering the logic that makes of them
(and me) confederates
of The Spider Girl, The Snake-skinned Man . . .

Poor devils have to live somehow.

I cross the boardwalk to the beach,
lie in the sand and gaze beyond
the clutter at the sea.

II
Trouble you for a light?
I turn as Aunt Jemima settles down
beside me, her blue-rinsed hair
without the red bandanna now.

I hold the lighter to her cigarette.
Much obliged. Unmindful (perhaps)
of my embarrassment, she looks
at me and smiles: You sure

do favor a friend I used to have.
Guess that's why I bothered you

for a light. So much like him that I—
She pauses, watching white horses rush

to the shore. Way them big old waves
come slamming whopping in,
sometimes it's like they mean to smash
this no-good world to hell.

Well, it could happen. A book I read—
Crossed that very ocean years ago.
London, Paris, Rome,
Constantinople too—I've seen them all.

Back when they billed me everywhere
as the Sepia High Stepper.
Crowned heads applauded me.
Years before your time. Years and years.

I wore me plenty diamonds then,
and counts or dukes or whatever they were
would fill my dressing room
with the costliest flowers. But of course

there was this one you resemble so.
Get me? The sweetest gentleman.
Dead before his time. Killed in the war
to save the world for another war.

High-stepping days for me
were over after that. Still I'm not one
to let grief idle me for long.
I went out with a mental act—

Jivin' Scribe, by Claude Clark, 1941.
(Collection of Reba and Dave Williams)

mind-reading—Mysteria From
The Mystic East—veils and beads
and telling suckers how to get
stolen rings and sweethearts back.

One night he was standing by my bed,
seen him plain as I see you,
and warned me without a single word:
Baby, quit playing with spiritual stuff.

So here I am, so here I am,
fake mammy to God's mistakes.
And that's the beauty part,
I mean, ain't that the beauty part.

She laughs, but I do not, knowing what
her laughter shields. And mocks.
I light another cigarette for her.
She smokes, not saying any more.

Scream of children in the surf,
adagios of sun and flashing foam,
the sexual glitter, oppressive fun. . . .
An antique etching comes to mind:

"The Sable Venus" naked on
a baroque Cellini shell—voluptuous
imago floating in the wake
of slave-ships on fantastic seas.

Jemima sighs, Reckon I'd best
be getting back. I help her up.
Don't you take no wooden nickels, hear?
Tin dimes neither. So long, pal.

THYLIAS MOSS

In "Landscape with Saxophonist," contemporary poet Thy-
lias Moss takes as her subject the age-old connection in Afri-
can-American culture between water and music. Like a
landscape painter, she assembles the "usual" props of
African-American musical performance: rain or the expec-

tation of it, the small animals who were once included in the
sacred circle, the cardplayers who people it now. Then she
sketches in the saxophonist, and the scene comes to life.
Although a beginner, the musician, like Sterling Brown's Ma
Rainey, has the power of wind and water. For those with the
patience to listen, "his playing moves the earth."

LANDSCAPE WITH SAXOPHONIST

The usual is there,
nondescript trees opened like umbrellas,
pessimists always expecting rain,
chickadees whose folding and unfolding wings
suggest the shuffling and reshuffling
of the cardsharp's deck;
nothing noteworthy except the beginning saxophonist
blowing with the efficacy of wolves addicted to pigs,
blowing down those poorly built houses,
the leaves off the trees, the water in
another direction, the ace of spades
into the ground with the cardsharp's bad intentions.
The discord and stridency set off landslides
and avalanches; his playing moves the earth
not lovers who are satisfied too quickly
and by the wrong things.

MICHAEL HARPER
No contemporary poet has written as often or as movingly
about African-American music as Michael Harper. Again

*and again, his work gives testimony to the unique achieve-
ments of jazz musicians like John Coltrane and Charlie
Parker: "Genius is undeniable, but genius is rare," Harper
has said. "When you see the real thing you know it, and you
don't need binoculars. . . . And that doesn't mean that you
can make it presentable; it doesn't even mean that you can
make it even sensible. But you can recognize what has
happened. . . . You can give testimony."*

*Of his own work, Harper has said, "my own poems are
very simply about belief." In this brief elegy for a son who
died at birth, Harper testifies to the enduring consolations of
"the music,* jazz.*"*

REUBEN, REUBEN

I reach from pain
to music great enough
to bring me back,
swollenhead, madness,
lovefruit, a pickle of hate
so sour my mouth twicked
up and would not sing;

there's nothing in the beat
to hold it in
melody and turn human skin;

a brown berry gone
to rot just two days on the branch;

we've lost a son,
the music, *jazz*, comes in.

Acknowledgments

James Baldwin: "Sonny's Blues." From "Sonny's Blues" collected in *Going to Meet the Man* © 1965. Copyright renewed. Reprinted with the permission of the James Baldwin Estate.

Toni Morrison: *Beloved*. Reprinted by permission of International Creative Management, Inc. Copyright 1987 by Toni Morrison.

Rita Dove: "The Musician Talks About Process" and *"Thomas at the Wheel."* "The Musician Talks About Process" first appeared in *Chelsea*, No. 49/1990. Copyright 1990 by Rita Dove. Reprinted by permission of the author.

"Thomas at the Wheel," from *Thomas and Beulah*. Copyright 1986 by Rita Dove. Reprinted by permission of the author.

Darryl Pinckney: "Equal Opportunities" from *High Cotton*. Copyright © 1992 by Darryl Pinckney. Reprinted by permission of Farrar, Straus & Giroux, Inc.

Andrea Lee: "New African." *Sarah Phillips* by Andrea Lee. Copyright © 1984 by Andrea Lee. Reprinted by permission of Random House.

Ralph Ellison: *Invisible Man*. *Invisible Man* by Ralph Ellison. Copyright © 1947, 1948, 1952 by Ralph Ellison. Reprinted by permission of Random House.

Samuel Allen: "A Moment, Please." *Soon, One Morning*, ed. Herbert Hill. Copyright © 1963 by Samuel Allen. Reprinted by permission of the author.

Ernest Gaines: "The Black Veil." *The Autobiography of Miss Jane Pittman* © 1971. Reprinted by permission of Bantam Doubleday Dell Publishing Group.

Charles Johnson: "Horace Bannon, Soulcatcher." *Oxherding Tale.* Reprinted by permission of Indiana University Press.

Marilyn Waniek: "Three Men in a Tent." *The Homeplace*, by Marilyn Nelson Waniek. Copyright © 1990 by the author, published by Louisiana State University Press. Used with permission.

Patricia Williams: *Alchemy of Race and Rights: Diary of a Law Professor.* Copyright © 1991 by Harvard University Press. Reprinted by permission of the publisher.

Samuel Delany: "The Man in the Wire-Filament Mask." *Stars in My Pocket Like Grains of Sand* by Samuel R. Delany. Copyright © 1984 by Samuel R. Delany. Used by permission of Bantam Books, a division of Bantam Doubleday Dell Publishing Group, Inc.

Connie Porter: "Mikey's New School." *All-Bright Court.* Copyright © 1991 by Connie Porter. Reprinted by permission of Houghton Mifflin Co. All rights reserved.

Jay Wright: "Veil, I." From *Elaine's Book.* Copyright © 1986 by Jay Wright. Reprinted by permission of the author.

Robert Hayden: "Aunt Jemima of the Ocean Waves" and *Middle Passage.* Reprinted from *Collected Poems* of Robert Hayden, edited by Frederick Glaysher, by permission of Liveright Publishing Corporation. Copyright © 1985 by Erma Hayden.

John Wideman: "Fever." Copyright © 1989 by John Wideman. Reprinted by permission of the author.

Jamaica Kincaid: "Leaving Home." Excerpt from "Poor Visitor" from *Lucy* by Jamaica Kincaid. Copyright © 1990 by Jamaica Kincaid. Reprinted by permission of Farrar, Straus & Giroux, Inc.

Calvin Forbes: "Blue Monday." Reprinted from *Blue Monday* © 1974 by Calvin Forbes, Wesleyan University. By permission of University Press of New England.

Michael Harper: "The Drowning of the Facts of a Life" and "Reuben, Reuben." Reprinted by permission of the author.

Derek Walcott, "The Shell's Howl." Excerpt from Chapter Twenty-Two from *Another Life* by Derek Walcott. Copyright © 1971, 1973 by Derek Walcott. Reprinted by permission of the author.

Melvin Dixon: "Grandmother: Crossing Jordan." This poem was reprinted by permission of the Estate of Melvin Dixon.

Christopher Gilbert: "This Bridge Across." Copyright by Christopher Gilbert. Reprinted from *Across the Mutual Landscape* with the permission of Graywolf Press, Saint Paul, Minnesota.

Langston Hughes: "The Negro Speaks of Rivers." *Selected Poems* by Langston Hughes. Copyright 1926 by Alfred A. Knopf, Inc. and renewed 1954 by Langston Hughes. Reprinted by permission of the publisher.

Richard Wright: "Uncle Hoskins." Excerpt from *Black Boy* by Richard Wright. Copyright 1937, 1942, 1944, 1945 by Richard Wright. Copyright renewed 1973 by Ellen Wright. Reprinted by permission of HarperCollins Publishers, Inc.

Sterling Brown: "Ma Rainey." All lines from "Ma Rainey" from *The Collected poems of Sterling A. Brown*, edited by Michael S. Harper. Copyright 1932 by Harcourt Brace & Co. Copyright renewed 1960 by Sterling A. Brown. Reprinted by permission of HarperCollins.

Gwendolyn Brooks: "Paul Robeson." *Blacks*. Published by Third World Press, 1991. Copyright © 1991 by Gwendolyn Brooks. Reprinted by permission of the author.

Audre Lorde: "The Day They Eulogized Mahalia." Reprinted from *Undersong, Chosen Poems Old and New*, revised edition, by Audre Lorde, by permission of W.W. Norton & Company, Inc.

Thylias Moss, "Landscape with Saxophonist." *Pyramid of Bone*, published by the University of Virginia Press, 1989. Reprinted by permission of the author.

Some Books by These Authors

Allen, Samuel
  Ivory Tusks, 1968
  Every Round and Other Poems, 1987

Baldwin, James
  Go Tell It on the Mountain, 1953
  Another Country, 1962
  Going to Meet the Man, 1965
  The Price of the Ticket: The Collected Non-Fiction, 1948–1985,
    1985

Brooks, Gwendolyn
  A Street in Bronzeville, 1945
  Annie Allen, 1949
  Maud Martha, a Novel, 1953
  Selected Poems, 1963
  Blacks, 1987

Brown, Sterling
  The Collected Poems of Sterling A. Brown, 1980

Delany, Samuel
  Neveryona, 1983
  Flight from Neveryona, 1984
  Stars in My Pocket Like Grains of Sand, 1985
  Return to Neveryona, 1994

Douglass, Frederick
  *Narrative of the Life of Frederick Douglass, an American Slave,
    Written by Himself*, 1845
  My Bondage and My Freedom, 1855

Dove, Rita
Fifth Sunday [stories], 1985
Thomas and Beulah, 1986
Through the Ivory Gate [novel], 1992
Selected Poems, 1994

Du Bois, W.E.B.
The Souls of Black Folk, 1903

Dunbar, Paul Laurence
The Collected Poetry of Paul Laurence Dunbar, 1993

Ellison, Ralph
Invisible Man, 1952
Shadow and Act [essays], 1964
Going to the Territory [essays], 1986

Forbes, Calvin
Blue Monday, 1974

Gaines, Ernest
Bloodline, 1968
The Autobiography of Miss Jane Pittman, 1971
A Lesson Before Dying, (1993)

Gilbert, Christopher
Across the Mutual Landscape, 1984

Harper, Michael
Dear John, Dear Coltrane, 1970
Nightmare Begins Responsibility, 1974
Images of Kin: New and Selected Poems, 1977
Healing Song for the Inner Ear, 1984

Hayden, Robert
Collected Prose, 1984
Collected Poems, 1985

Hughes, Langston
  The Langston Hughes Reader, 1958
  Selected Poems, 1959

Jacobs, Harriet
  *Incidents in the Life of a Slave Girl:
  Written by Herself*, 1861

Johnson, Charles
  Oxherding Tale, 1982
  The Sorcerer's Apprentice, 1986
  Middle Passage, 1990

Kincaid, Jamaica
  Annie John, 1985
  A Small Place, 1988
  Lucy, 1990

Lee, Andrea
  Russian Journal, 1981
  Sarah Phillips, 1984

Lorde, Audre
  The Black Unicorn, 1978
  Zami: A New Spelling of My Name [autobiography], 1982
  A Burst of Light: Essays, 1988
  Undersong: Chosen Poems, Old and New, 1992

Morrison, Toni
  The Bluest Eye, 1969
  Sula, 1973
  Song of Solomon, 1977
  Beloved, 1988

Moss, Thylias
  Pyramid of Bone, 1988
  Rainbow Remnants in Rock Bottom Ghetto Sky, 1991

Pinckney, Darryl
High Cotton, 1992

Porter, Connie
All-Bright Court, 1992

Walcott, Derek
Dream on Monkey Mountain [plays], 1970
Another Life, 1973
Collected Poems: 1948–1984, 1986
Omeros, 1990

Waniek, Marilyn
Mama's Promises, 1985
The Homeplace, 1990

Wideman, John
Brothers and Keepers (autobiography), 1984
The Homewood Trilogy, 1985
Fever: Twelve Stories, 1989
The Stories of John Edgar Wideman, 1992

Williams, Patricia
*The Alchemy of Race and Rights:
Diary of a Law Professor*, 1991

Wright, Jay
Selected Poems, 1987
Elaine's Book, 1988
Boleros, 1991

Wright, Richard
Uncle Tom's Children: Four Novellas, 1940
Native Son, 1940
Black Boy, 1945
Eight Men, 1961

Index

Page numbers in *italics* refer to illustrations.

157